TO THE CHILDREN OF MAINE

MY NATIVE STATE

THE AUTHOR INSCRIBES THIS BOOK

Twenty Years at Pemaquid

Sketches of Its History and Its Remains

Ancient and Modern

M A I N E

J. Henry Cartland

The restless sea resounds along the shore,
The light land breeze flows outward with a sigh,
And each to each seems chanting evermore
A mournful memory of the days gone by:
All underneath these tufted mounds of grass
Lies many a relic, many a storied stone,
And pale ghosts rise as lingering footsteps pass
The ruined fort with tangled vines o'ergrown.
—*Mrs. M. W. Hackelton.*

HERITAGE BOOKS
2023

HERITAGE BOOKS
AN IMPRINT OF HERITAGE BOOKS, INC.

Books, CDs, and more—Worldwide

For our listing of thousands of titles see our website
at
www.HeritageBooks.com

A Facsimile Reprint
Published 2023 by
HERITAGE BOOKS, INC.
Publishing Division
5810 Ruatan Street
Berwyn Heights, MD 20740

Originally published
Pemaquid Beach, Maine
1914

— Publisher's Notice —
In reprints such as this, it is often not possible to remove blemishes from the original. We feel the contents of this book warrant its reissue despite these blemishes and hope you will agree and read it with pleasure.

International Standard Book Number
Paperbound: 978-0-7884-2707-7

INTRODUCTION.

Many an ancient spot, rendered dear by tradition and sacred associations, is disguised by a modern aspect. But though time brushes away the old landmarks and the once familiar scenes disappear, the halo cast by memory remains, and the locality lives in our hearts and thoughts as it was before the change. REV. DR. T. DEWITT TALMAGE.

Many people visit Old Pemaquid every year who have once claimed it as their home, but have been obliged to seek employment elsewhere. Few visit this place who do not wish to come again to enjoy its attractive natural scenery and try to fathom the hidden mysteries of its past.

After one year of research here I thought it would be an easy task to write a history of Pemaquid. To-day after many years of investigation I have changed my mind. It is not from lack of interesting material, but it has been difficult to select the most interesting facts and put them in the most attractive form. I am especially indebted to Rev. H. O. Thayer of Portland, Maine, for valuable aid in compiling this work and for translations of important French documents; also to Miss Bell, a lady from Canada, a good French scholar, who made her home here at the Jamestown Hotel, I am indebted for translations of French documents and other useful information. From Prof. John Johnston's History of Bristol and Bremen, which has been very freely quoted in this work, I have obtained more information than from any other single volume. Others, too numerous to mention, have contributed a sketch, a poem, a story, or bits of history,— to all of whom I tender my hearty thanks.

past history, as well as much mystery, which yet puzzles, while it interests the antiquarian. No naturalist has yet solved the mystery of the great oyster shell mounds of Ancient Pemaquid on the Damariscotta River, or historian, of the excellent pavings found at three different localities on both banks of the Pemaquid River; thousands of other relics are objects of interest to the traveler.

The Eastern Steamship Corporation have two steamers running from Portland; the "Monhegan," of the Portland and Rockland line, which touches at New Harbor, and the Boothbay line, for Boothbay Harbor, South Bristol and East Boothbay. New Harbor and South Bristol are both near Pemaquid and easily reached from either place. These steamers connect at Portland with boats from New York and Boston. At Bath the Kennebec line from Boston connects with the steamers "Southport" and "Westport" for Boothbay Harbor and Pemaquid direct, daily in summer. A smaller excursion boat called the "Tourist," connects with all the summer resorts in the vicinity of Pemaquid several times each day.

The steamer Newcastle, Capt. E. P. Gamage, for Damariscotta and way stations, and the steamer Islesford, Capt. Plummer Leeman, for Boothbay Harbor and way stations, from South Bristol, make two trips daily.

There are two steamer landings at Pemaquid, the first is called PEMAQUID BEACH; the second PEMAQUID HARBOR, which lies across the river, on the west side. Passengers for the Penny Cottages, Edgemere Hotel, Bayview House, Lookout Cottage and Pemaquid Falls, land at the latter. Those passengers wishing to reach Long Cove, New Harbor, Pemaquid Point, the Beach or Jamestown Hotel, near the landing, leave at the first station, where carriages are ready to convey them to their respective destinations.

The landing called Pemaquid Beach is near the ruins of the Old Fort, marked by the Old Fort Rock of Pemaquid with date of 1607 upon it. This date is to commemorate the landing of the Popham Colony, the first English people at this place, on August 8th and 10th, 1607.

This was thirteen years previous to the Plymouth Colony at Cape Cod. They had two ships and one hundred and twenty people. One ship, the "Mayflower," brought one hundred and two passengers, Dec., 1620; the ship "Newport," brought one hundred and five to Jamestown, May 6th, 1607.

This rock is now surrounded by the Old Castle restored on the original foundations and most of the original stone of which it was first built, by Sir William Phips, in 1692. This foundation, discovered in 1893, was found to be in good condition, after being buried and forgotten since the American Revolution of 1775.

Here, also, is the Old Fort House, its beautiful peninsula, with its "field of graves," the site of the ancient capital of Pemaquid with its paved streets, which have been buried for centuries and only discovered by accident, and the great white sand beach with its continued "music of the sea;" also smaller beaches, the wonderful collection of curios and antiques, telling their undisputable stories of a people of long ago, who had become almost forgotten by their successors to this favored home of those who "go down to the sea in ships."

CHAPTER I.

Location of Pemaquid

ALTHOUGH once the most noted locality by far of all New England, to-day comparatively few people know anything of Pemaquid, its location, its topography or formation, or its history.

Pemaquid as known to-day embraces three natural divisions of the southern part of the town of Bristol in Lincoln County, Maine. Bristol is bounded on the west by the Damariscotta River, on the north by the town of that name, and Bremen, once a part of Bristol, on the east and south by Broad Sound, the ocean and John's Bay. John's River on the west and Pemaquid River on the east divide the lower section into three parts, consisting of high ridges of land which lie between them.

Bristol derived its name from a noted city of that name in England, whose leading merchants were among the first to manifest a deep interest in American discovery, and subscribed a thousand pounds to fit out an expedition in 1603 to explore and trade on the New England coast. It was once on the highway of travel, when sailing vessels necessarily visited land often for fresh supplies of fuel and water. Now larger and swifter ships propelled by steam, race across the Atlantic Ocean in less days than it then took weeks, and the passing immigrant or traveler is rushed on to the more southern and western parts of our country, leaving the varied attractions of our State unseen, and by many unknown.

As the great lines of ships pass us on the one side, so the lines of railroads transport their passengers upon the other,

Pemaquid Harbor, from the Bay View House, at the Mouth of Pemaquid River

leaving old Pemaquid neglected while its inhabitants seek a livelihood on the very site of its ruins, former paved streets, and fortifications. All along the sea coast which bounds the southern shore of Maine, are many points, or peninsulas varying in length and height, and islands, which are all caused by nature's upheaval of mineral formation, the unbroken parts forming its peninsulas, and those rising out of the ocean at their southern extremities, the beautiful islands for which this coast has been noted since its first discovery by the white man. These divisions of land have been compared to the fingers of one's hand, between which, flow bays and rivers of salt and fresh water. Across the head waters of the bays in this section, to save expensive bridging, the railroad extends direct from Bath to Rockland, thus spanning the territory of Pemaquid, east and west, and which — bounded by the Kennebec and Penobscot — was claimed formerly by both the French and the English. On the south it was bounded by the broad ocean, on the north, or land side, indefinitely. Not a pound of railroad iron has ever been laid in Bristol to bring travel to our shores, the whistle of the locomotive or the rattle of the electric car never startled our deer or other wild game, and the telephone had never stretched out its hand to greet us till the year 1898. Teams and stages convey the mail, goods and people by land, as formerly, and sailing vessels and small steamers by water, as in times past.

Within the last decade the tide of travel to some extent has turned back "down east" and many people come this way where, for generations past, they have had the reputation of "prying up the sun in the morning." Portland, with its noted isles of Casco Bay; Fort Popham, Boothbay, Squirrel and Heron Islands, Christmas Cove, South Bristol and Pemaquid, and so on to Bar Harbor; and beyond are resorts on our shores now eagerly sought by increasing thousands every year. Historians and lovers of the antique seek Pemaquid, where they find, besides many attractions of other sorts, a locality rich in

CHAPTER II.

Pemaquid as it Appears Today

FOR further description of Pemaquid it seems necessary to note the present appearance, and industries of its people. As most people visit this place by water, I will join the traveler at Boothbay, with his permission, and point out the various places of interest as we journey to the former capital, now called Pemaquid Beach, located at the mouth of the Pemaquid River. As we stand on the deck, or gaze from the cabin window of one of the steamers daily plying between Boothbay and this place in the summer, many places of interest can be seen to good advantage.

The first large island we pass on the right hand is "Squirrel," well known as a summer resort all along the New England coast, having a fine hotel and well dotted over with many cottages of summer visitors. Steamers and naphtha boat landings are frequent there from Boothbay and vicinity. On the opposite side we pass the wide entrance to Linekin's Bay; on the high land at the north end we plainly see the three villages of Bayville, Murray Hill and Paradise, where many people from Massachusetts find a pleasant residence during the summer months, kept comfortable by the cool sea breezes which come across the bay from the broad ocean. On the southern point at the eastern entrance of this bay we see the dark, spruce-covered land called Nigger Island, and the pretty clustering summer cottages of the new settlement named Ocean Point. Then, as we enter the mouth of the Damariscotta River, close by on the right, we see the government lighthouse and fog bell

Captain Alfred Race

of Ram Island; the next in line, extending south is Fishermans, and the outer one, Damariscove Island (called in times past Damerills). That has a very small harbor at the south end where a life-saving station is located.

In 1676 when King Philip sent his emissaries along the coast of New England to annihilate the white settlers, the inhabitants of Pemaquid fled in terror from their homes, and three hundred of them gathered on Damariscove Island, and from there watched the smoking ruins of their former homes as they were being destroyed by the flaming torch of the savages. Here, too, in olden times the rollicking and jolly English fisherman celebrated his home customs by dancing around the May-pole to song and instrumental music. In this group those high islands lying a little farther east are rightly named White Islands, as their rocky shores show white from the evergreen trees on their heights to the water boundary of the sea below. The Hypocrites, Pumpkin Islands and Outer Heron Island are others of this group.

Many stories of ghosts, hidden treasures and pirates have been told of the latter island, legends that still cling to many a spot along our rugged coast. On Outer Heron Island was kept, a few years ago, a colony of imported foxes, which were cared for by their owner, Capt. R. H. Emerson, a veteran of the civil war, carrying many scars of battle. Several fishermen kept him company, and on the surrounding islands others have their homes in close proximity to excellent fishing grounds. The veteran has passed to his long home and the colony of foxes was not a success.

Passing on to Inner Heron where we land at the northern end, we are fairly among the great group of islands sometimes called the "Archipelago of Pemaquid." All the land we now see about us is surrounded by water except that lying across the river just west of us, and it could also be made an island by digging a canal a few hundred feet long.

Inner Heron Island, a noted health resort, has a charming

location directly in the mouth or outlet of the Damariscotta River, where it is a mile wide. Its hotel, the Madockawando, is named for a Chief of the Penobscot tribe whose daughter married the French officer, Baron de Castine. The majority of the summer visitors upon this island are from western Massachusetts.

While the steamer lies here at the wharf of Heron Island we can take a view up the river for several miles, the banks of which are quite high and well covered with evergreen trees. Some account of the history connected with it may prove interesting.

A short way up this river are the two villages known as South Bristol on the left bank, and East Boothbay across the river on the right bank. These two villages, having no railroads, were formerly connected with Portland and several other places, by steamer "Enterprise," and Captain Race and his officers and men, so well and favorably known along our sea coast. The Eastern Steamship Corporation purchased the "Enterprise" in June, 1912, and took her off the route, but very wisely secured the services of Captain Race and his people to command the steamer succeeding her.

This is a salt-water river, so-called because its shores are bounded by the high ridges of rocks, ledges and soil, such as abound along our Maine sea coast, confining the tidewaters of the ocean in the form of rivers, bays and beautiful coves which form such fine harbors and give access to vessels far into the land. Up this river the tide ebbs and flows swiftly for fourteen miles, where a large lake flows into it over a steep embankment and gives fine water power for electric lights for miles distant.

Here millions of fish called alewives gather every spring and by struggling hard, gain the fresh water of the lake above, where they deposit their eggs to hatch, returning to the salt water in a few weeks. Their young, on attaining a length of about three inches, follow their parents to the ocean and go

Steamer Enterprise at Boothbay Harbor

south like the mackerel, porgie, dog fish, shad and many others. Where they pass the winter no man knows, but this we know: some fish, when they go south are fat and in fine condition but when they return in the spring are lean and poor. Like the migratory birds, they seek a more congenial climate in winter than ours. It has always been a puzzle, a remarkable law of nature, that a fish should be able to exist a part of its life in salt water and a part in fresh water, and that the fish of the great salt ocean should have to seek the fresh water lakes to propogate their young.

The first landing place, called South Bristol, is on the left bank of this river, at the north end of Rutherford Island. This name is said to have been given it by Rev. Robert Rutherford, a Presbyterian clergyman who came to Pemaquid as chaplain for David Dunbar, who was sent to rebuild Fort Frederic in 1729. A bridge joins the island to the mainland. Two summer hotels, the Summit House, kept by Mr. Nelson Gamage, and the Thompson Inn, kept by E. McFarland, are well patronized by a fine class of people, many of them Friends, or Quakers, from Philadelphia. A postoffice, stores, a shipyard and many summer cottages are located there. The next village two miles distant across the river is East Boothbay, (formerly Hodgdon's Mills from the large tide-mill there). Vessels of large dimensions were formerly built there, but today are built principally fine steam and sailing yachts, naptha boats by the Rice Brothers, and fine fishing craft by the Hodgdon Brothers and Mr. Adams.

Passing up the river, on Fort Island are the ruins of Fort Farley at its south end. The other places of interest along the banks of this river are establishments where a great quantity of ice is cut principally from artificial fresh water ponds, on both banks of the river. Bricks, hay and wood are other articles of export. The transportation by large vessels plying up and down the river, often propelled by towboats, form interesting pictures which add to its attraction. Brick yards were numerous on the banks of this river forty years ago, and many ships were built there by people who lived in the vicinity, and in the towns about were men who could navigate and sail them around the world.

Twelve miles from its mouth are the quiet and pretty twin villages of Damariscotta and Newcastle, one on either bank of the river, joined by a substantial iron bridge. Two miles farther up the river, are found the famous Oyster Shell Mounds, a puzzle to the naturalist and investigator since first discovered by the white settlers, where yet remain immense heaps of decomposing shells from two to twenty-five feet deep, covering acres of ground on both banks of the river, and in some places are found ten feet deep in the bed of the bay. In the October number of the New England Magazine, 1898, is to be found an excellent illustrated sketch pertaining to those mounds, written by George Stillman Berry.

We now continue our trip to Pemaquid. The next landing is the pretty little harbor of Christmas Cove, thought by some to have been named by the Norsemen when they visited our shores in 1001. It might be well to cherish this name in remembrance of their visits to our New England coast. There are hieroglyphical inscriptions found upon rocks at Monhegan and Damariscove Islands, supposed by many to have been the work of the Norsemen, but we do not consider them reliable. We have abundant historical evidence of their visits to our shores centuries before Columbus came here, and records recently found at the Vatican, by Mr. John B. Shipley, show that the Roman Church had in its possession a map furnished by them of New England and the eastern coast of North America, fifty years before the Columbus Expedition, showing that their discovery was recorded at that time. It is strange if Columbus, as well as some other mariners of his time, did not learn of it long before he sailed for America. In 1892 a Viking ship, a model of one of those used a thousand years ago, passed these shores on its way to the World's Fair at Chicago.

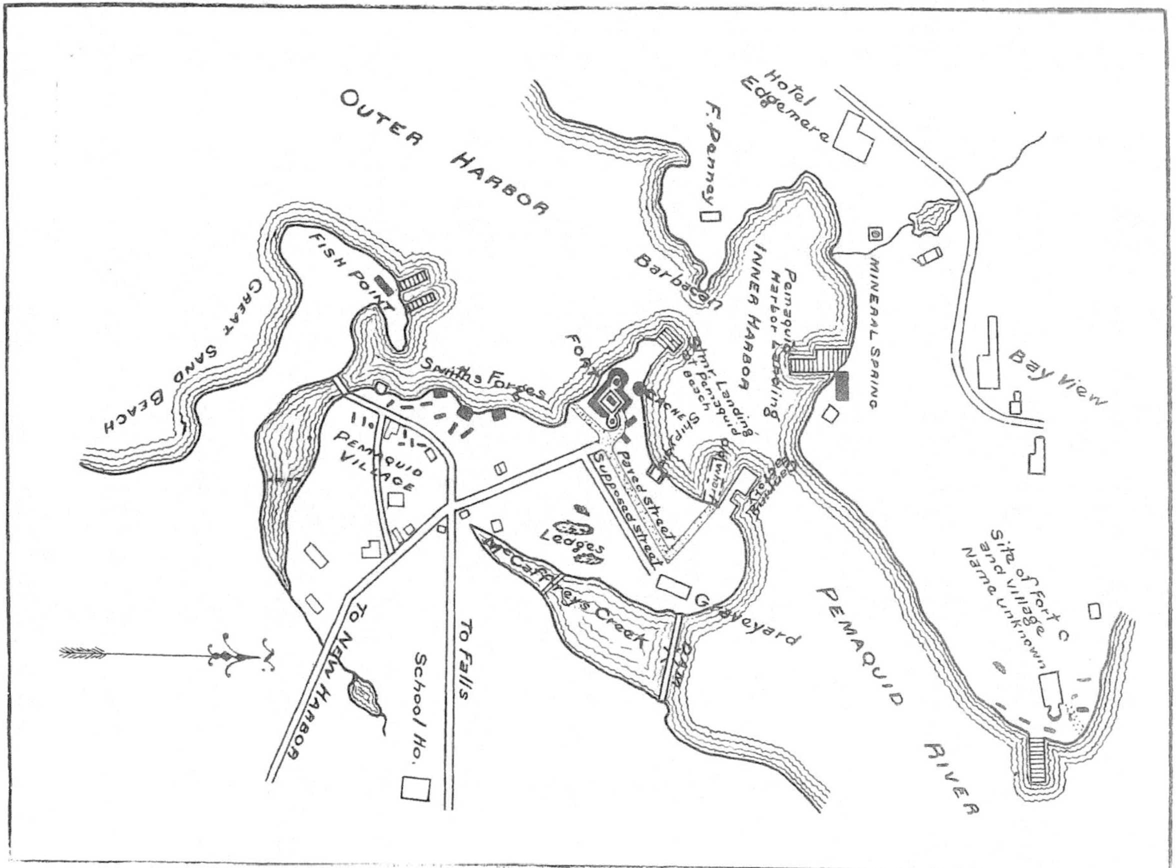

Plan of Pemaquid Harbor and Vicinity, Showing the Sites of the Forts on Both Sides of the River

The story of those hardy men, pictures, and descriptions of their ships propelled by oars and a single square sail, make interesting reading. We have a fine engraving of one of them on exhibition at the museum in the restored castle at Pemaquid. "All the monarchs of England after William the Conqueror, himself the grandson of a Sea King, are descendants of the hardy Norsemen. They wore hoods upon their heads, surmounted with eagles' wings and walruses' tusks, mailed armor, and for robes the skins of polar bears. In the following old ballad their hardy and ferocious disposition is well portrayed."

"He scorns to rest 'neath the smoky rafter,
He plows with his boat the roaring deep;
The billows boil and the storm howls after—
But the tempest is only a thing of laughter—
The sea-king loves it better than sleep!"

They deserve a passing notice here because we of English descent can trace our ancestry back to the Norsemen who overrun England under William the Conqueror.

Not many years ago Christmas Cove was one of the many fishing stations located along our coast from which sailed large and substantial fishing vessels, with sturdy crews, on long voyages to the banks of Newfoundland and other places. The Thorpe brothers, owning two vessels, one called the "Mountain Laurel" sailed by Capt. Edward, and the "Twilight," by Capt. Loring Thorpe, used to belong here. They made two trips to the banks for codfish each spring, being gone from six to eight weeks; then during the latter part of the summer visited the Bay of Chaleurs and British coast in pursuit of mackerel. Large buildings were required to store and salt the fish they caught, and flakes covering much land were built to dry and cure them on. A store was provided to furnish goods to the families of those hardy men who manned their vessels. This is one of the "passing industries" of our sea coast. Steamers now land passengers where old bankers landed codfish. The old storehouses protect the freight and baggage of the summer visitors, and the descendants of the fishermen cater to their wants. A large hotel, the Holly Inn, is located there, that will accommodate about two hundred people, and is kept by Albert Thorpe.

As we pass out of Christmas Cove, continuing our passage toward Pemaquid Beach, we leave Inner Heron Island on the south. The large island which the steamer heads for, whose highest part is covered with spruce trees, is called Thrumbcap. It is owned by Mr. Edward C. Holmes, (a relative of Oliver Wendell Holmes) who, with his family and friends, have occupied it for several years, using steam and sailing yachts for conveyance to different places of interest. One of the prettiest little beaches to be found in this section extends across a cove at the south end of this island, which consists entirely of finely broken and bleached mussel shells. Mr. Holmes has shipped many barrels of those found about the island for hens. At one time he had a mill at one of the oyster shell heaps, above referred to, on the eastern bank of the Damariscotta River, where he made a business of grinding up the shells for the same purpose.

Here we change our course, abruptly sweeping around the black spar buoy on our left and entering a narrow passage called the "Thread of Life," which is formed by a part of the smaller islands, which extend in nearly a straight line between the two larger islands: Thrumbcap on the south, and Birch Island on the north. The little huts seen along this passage upon either side of it, are occupied, a part of the year, by fishermen who come from a distance to catch lobsters, finding a safe and convenient harbor for the pursuit of their occupation.

Leaving this passage we then pass a red buoy on the right, at the north end of Crow Island, and enter the southern part of John's Bay. A few years ago a small cottage was built on this little island and occupied by Mr Fred Partridge and Mr. Henry Sproul, both belonging to Pemaquid Beach, but who were engaged in their occupation of catching lobsters here.

This was more convenient to the fishing grounds, and saved them a long row morning and evening to and from their work. There were no power boats then. A severe easterly gale came on one night, and Mr. Sproul's boat filled with water as it lay at the mooring, and the mast and sail went adrift. Mr. Sproul took a small skiff and rowed out and got it, but while rowing back one of the rowlocks came out, forcing him to leave the sail and return to the shore for another, which Mr. Partridge gave him. By this time the sail had drifted quite a distance, and after reaching it, for some reason he gave up trying to save the sail and started to row back very fast, as though his skiff had begun to fill, or it was too rough for him. Again the rowlock came out, which made him tip to one side of the skiff and capsize. Not being able to swim he quickly sunk from view, weighted down, as he was, with heavy oil clothes and rubber boots. Mr. Partridge could do nothing to assist him, and so spent the most lonesome and dubious night he had ever experienced, made worse by the storm of snow and wind that prevailed. At daylight he hoisted a blanket in a spruce tree and started a fire beside it, which attracted the attention of Mr. Thorpe and another man on the island adjoining, who came to his relief. The people soon began dragging for the body of the drowned man, and secured it with a troll of fish hooks.

Several people have been drowned in this vicinity since the writer came here in 1888: Henry Sproul, William McClain and Leforest Curtis, a man and boy up Johns River—Mr. Almond D. McClain and Harold McClain, and Ralph Stevens.

Another event which occurred here about fifty years ago may be worth recording. At that time and long previously the fishermen along the shore used many small vessels, fishing for the most part at night, and taking their catch on shore and salting them in "butts," as the hogsheads they used were called, where they would remain in pickle until the fall, when they would be taken out and dried on flakes, ready for market. When they were cured they were put on board their vessels and taken to market, usually to Portland from this locality, and then all hands would have a grand good time visiting the theatres and other shows, purchase their provisions and other articles that pleased their fancy, then return to their homes to enjoy the fruits of their summer labor. A former Captain of Pemaquid, named Charles Geyer, with two of his sons, had made their usual summer trip to Portland and were returning, but when within three miles of their home, and owing to a severe storm which had been raging, a heavy sea was breaking over the shallow places all along the shore, and at the entrance of the passage called "the thread of life" the sea, at intervals, would break entirely across, to the opposite shore. Just as they arrived here a heavy wave met them and dashed their vessel on the jagged rocks, ending her career. The people escaped in their small boat, losing nearly everything which they had purchased. Mr. John Geyer had bought a violin to amuse himself with through the long winter evenings. As they rowed up the bay towards their home Mr. Charles Geyer, turning to his son, made this inquiry of him: "John, what kind of a tune do you suppose your fiddle is playing now?" He was a man who had lost one hand by the bursting of a gun and did not seem to let small affairs ruffle his temper.

The following story, copied from the Boothbay Register of March 14, 1914, illustrates well what I have heard the old fishermen tell of their early voyages when they had to do all their cooking over open fire places as was done both on vessels and on shore before stoves and ranges were invented. To-day they sail in larger vessels that employ from twelve to twenty men. Many of these vessels are equipped with naptha power and have the most up-to-date appliances for cooking and the best "grub" the market affords, to which the men do justice by eating four meals a day when business is good.

"A veteran fisherman writes of his first trip to the banks as cook. Sixty-two years ago, when sixteen years of age, he shipped on a schooner of forty tons. 'She had a brick fire place to cook with. My wages were eight dollars a month. The skipper was twenty-one years old and his brother was eighteen. The crew of four men have all gone to rest. Some difference in fitting up then than now; no butter, no sugar, but plenty of hardtack. I cooked a few meals before leaving home just to get my hand in. The skipper's brother asked me to cook some rice. I asked him 'how much?' he says, 'oh, four mugs full.' I put it on to boil. The first I noticed was the cover rising up. I took half of it out and set it going again, but soon the cover was up again. I took out more and filled every dish in the galley with rice. The skipper looked down and exclaimed, 'for G–d sake what are you doing with all that rice? We can never eat it.' Nothing to burn but candles. I had a Dutch oven to bake bread in. One of the crew showed me how to make a dandy bunk. I had to roast and grind my own coffee. When we left for the Cape Sables the men were all full of rum and molasses, they could hardly steer the vessel. The skipper pointed out a star to steer for. The man at the wheel yelled out that he had lost the star, but we got to the fishing ground and caught a good fare of fish and returned home all safe.' "

In the far distance we catch a glimpse of that "Grand Isle of the Sea," called Monhegan, an Indian name having the accent on the second syllable, like Men-an-as, Mus-con-gus, Na-han-a-da, etc. This name is composed of two Indian words, "Men-a-han." an island, and "Ki-gan," land in or by the great sea, meaning island at sea, or great sea island. [This definition by R. K. Sewall, author of Ancient Dominions of Maine.]

This island is important on account of its connection with the early history of Pemaquid, being the one first mentioned in connection with it. For several years past it has been sought as a quiet retreat by artists and other people from the cities. Capt. William S. Humphrey with his schooner "Effort" used to transport the passengers and mail to and from Boothbay

Harbor. The "Effort" was blown up by gasolene a few years ago and now passengers, freight and the mail are carried daily between the island and the main by the steamer May Archer, Capt. Isaac Archibald. For ages this great island has stood like a sentinel to direct the incoming mariner to the mouth of the Penobscot River, as our other noted island of Seguin has always been the guide to the Kennebec. There are now powerful lights on each of those islands to guide the mariners at night while sailing in all directions about them.

The nearest land seen across the bay which forms its western boundary is Pemaquid Point, about three miles in length, on which stands another government lighthouse and large fog bell, formerly attended by Charles A. Dolliver and Herman E. Brewer. It is now attended by Mr. E. E. Marr and his family. This lighthouse was established and first attended in 1824 by Mr. Isaac Dunham, whose grandson, Martin V. B. Dunham, now has a fine summer cottage and owns the little island at the entrance of New Harbor, the northeastern boundary of that point. This point is an excellent specimen of those finger-like projections spoken of in the preceding chapter, sloping from the high ridge along its center to the shore in all directions. This, like most of the other points and islands in this vicinity, is now partially covered with a thick growth of spruce and fir trees, which have taken the place of large pines and other growth, which, centuries ago, existed here. Capt. John Smith, when he surveyed this coast in 1614, wondered how such large trees could grow upon the islands and main in this vicinity. Along the high ridges of these peninsulas extend excellent roads, with branches leading in various directions to the shore. Many fine fields and pastures, with the homes of their owners, are scattered all over this locality, forming an attractive scene.

An interesting fact connected with this point is that for many years past a large flock of sheep, ranging from one to three hundred in number, belonging to the Partridge heirs, have obtained their living on the western shore of this point

Self-supporting Sheep. For Many Years Mr. Partridge kept Hundreds of these Sheep on Pemaquid Point

of land. I am informed by Mr. Partridge that they had not been fed for many years past, until soon after the great storm of Nov. 26, 1898, he had a small load of hay hauled down to them. This was the great easterly gale in which the steamship City of Portland was lost, when her passengers, of over two hundred, perished, attempting to reach Portland from Boston. At Pemaquid, the schooner H. H. Chamberlain, with four young men on board, was blown out of the harbor and away south to the Gulf Stream. Their people despaired of ever seeing them again but they returned after two weeks' suffering from their dangerous voyage. I visited the feeding ground of the sheep just a few days afterwards, and the hay was still there, while they were eating the food nature had supplied them with. They know when the tide leaves the shore at low water as well as a person; they go in flocks to seek their food, eating the dulse and other vegetation thrown up by the sea. At high water they feed upon the moss and evergreen foliage found on the shore. Among the thickest clusters of spruce trees they find their only protection from the howling blasts of winter, and this growth is so thick that no ray of sunshine can penetrate in summer. They lived and thrived with little care or expense to their owners. This industry is now done away with as the sheep became troublesome to their owners on account of bad dogs, and also an annoyance to summer visitors and others having gardens to protect.

On Sept. 17, 1903, a heavy gale occurred here in the night, by which two vessels were wrecked within one-fourth of a mile of each other, at the end of Pemaquid Point. The first was the George F. Edmonds, Capt. Willard Pool, a large fisherman from Boston, with seventeen men on board, fifteen of whom were drowned, including the captain, whose body was not recovered until the following spring. One of the men saved, Mr. John Lewis, lived only to perish with cold the next winter in Boston Bay, while in an open dory on a fishing trip. The other vessel was a coaster from Boston, the Sadie and

Lillie, Capt. Harding, who lost his life, the crew being saved. We have relics from both vessels at the Museum at Pemaquid Beach. Many vessels and hardy sailors have ended their career in this vicinity since the old Archangel perished here in 1635, the first to be cast away on the New England coast.

As we sail out into Johns Bay from the "Thread of Life," we have sailed nearly around the village of Christmas Cove, giving us a fine view of the rough, rugged sea-washed coast, dotted over with many fine summer cottages, and the large hotel called the Holly Inn, all very conspicuous by their high elevation upon the solid rock foundation of this island.

Another very beautiful island now comes in view, which belongs to a school teacher who resides in Somerville, Mass., on which is a fine cottage that she occupies during her summer vacation. This is called Birch Island on account of the many white birch trees growing upon it. Between this long, narrow island and Rutherfords is a splendid sheet of water, (called by some the "Grave Yard,") where small boats can lay the year round in perfect safety from all storms that may rage just beyond it, in the Bay. At the south end of the harbor is a thick growth of trees and bushes named the "Heron's Nest." To fully enjoy this beautiful land-locked sheet of water one should enter it at the north end, near the Holly Inn and sail or row through the whole length of it, coming out at the narrow passage at the north end into Johns Bay. At low water its natural beauty is to be seen at the best advantage, as the water is shallow so the rough rocks and ledges and a variety of sea vegetation and many fish are to be seen.

As we pass Birch Island on our left we come in view of the most conspicuous part of Rutherfords Island, called Otis Head. This high, rugged shore, with its rough granite ledges, boulders and sturdy evergreen trees, with landlocked creeks and coves, all form an interesting place to visit. From a great square tower on the summit of this hill a grand view of the surrounding scenery is to be had. This has been erected recently by Mr. Samuel A. Miles, of New York City, who, by his efforts of the past eight years, has been gradually adding to this spot of natural beauty by erecting a fine mansion on the summit, building roads to the north and south to connect with the steamer landings at Christmas Cove and South Bristol. He has ornamented the roadways and other accessible spots with thrifty fruit trees and rare flowers, giving many people employment in that vicinity.

As we sail straight across the bay toward the large island seen ahead called Johns Island, (named by Capt. John Smith, also the bay and village, when he came here in 1614, appointed Admiral of New England,) we have a clear view for several miles up the bay on the west side which, as it grows narrower, is called Johns River to distinguish it from the wider portion near the ocean. On its western shores are places that have figured principally in the past history of Pemaquid as well as those figuring in its present. The first place of interest above Otis Head is a narrow passageway called the "Gut." This waterway forms the northern boundary of Rutherfords Island, some half mile in length, connecting this bay with the Damariscotta River, before mentioned, which boats and small steamers often traverse on their way from one village to another on these shores, South Bristol being located at the farther entrance, and Witch Island, formerly called Davis, at the east entrance.

A small island lies just south of Witch, now the summer home of Mr. Broughton of Massachusetts, and was formerly owned by "Uncle Tommy Gamage," whose wife named it the "Little Gem." He with his little row boat used to ferry commercial travelers and others, across the bay to Pemaquid and other villages, before naphtha boats and steamers were introduced into these waters. Witch Island contains about 16 acres of well wooded land and, in connection with Little Gem, is so located that it forms a good harbor at the east end of this passage. It has been owned since 1887 by Mr. Daniel Chittenden, "Uncle Dan," and his wife, Grace Courtland, called the "Witch of Wall Street," of New York City, as she was at one time financial editor of the Wall Street Daily News, and Uncle Dan was connected with another journal there.

About forty years ago there was quite an extensive business carried on at this place, that of trying out small fish called Porgies, or Menhaden, once very numerous on the coast of Maine during the summer months, and depended upon for bait by the fishermen to catch larger fish. They were caught in great numbers and tried out for the oil and scrap they furnished, the oil being used in dressing leather and mixing with paint oil, and the scrap to mix in fertilizers. Now those fish seldom come this way further than Cape Cod. There were five establishments for trying out the oil located at this place. Today there are but slight indications of this former industry: a few stumps of former wharf piling and some of the stone foundations of the buildings are all that are now visible. Many other places along the Maine coast where this business once flourished and the inhabitants thrived by it are abandoned, the factories and wharves fallen into decay and the steamers and their crews who made the business lively, have followed the industry to more southern waters, where they still find employment as captains, pilots, engineers and cooks on the many boats in the business there.

The next point of interest is just beyond Witch Island. At the head of a little cove is an old burying ground walled in with roughly laid stone, so thickly overgrown with large trees in and about the yard that it cannot be seen from the water's edge. An investigation will show that of about one hundred graves marked mostly by natural, rough stones, but very few have any names or dates to indicate who were laid there. I have been informed by aged people living in this vicinity that in ancient times people were carried in boats from Pemaquid

A Load of Porgies at Pemaquid

to this place for burial. All about the head of this cove are located summer cottages built by Mr. King.

Passing on to the next cove, called McFarland's, we find one of the pretty little nooks and corners for which old Pemaquid is noted; — a sand and pebble beach, a verdant field sloping to the sunny south, at the water's edge grass-covered mounds of crumbling shells from which have been taken bones of the Indian and wild animals, with many fine implements of the former; — a boat shop operated by Addison McFarland, and several dwelling houses, the pleasant homes of the present settlers and a few summer visitors. This pretty little cove, beach and field are bounded on the east and west by ridges of upheaved granitic ledges, partially covered with soil and vegetation.

The next high land up the river is called High Island. A large lobster pound is located there, owned by Capt. Isaac Harvey, of Boston. There is another on the opposite side of the river, formerly operated by Capt. Alexander Kennedy, and now owned by the United States Government and used to retain egg, or seed lobsters until the eggs mature, which requires about eleven months from the time of depositing on the flipperets by the mother. They cling there as though glued, to the number of from fifteen to sixty thousand. When nearly matured the lobsters are taken to the Government Hatchery at Boothbay Harbor, the eggs stripped off, and after bursting their shells, are distributed along the sea coast by the small steamer Gannett, Capt. Geo. Greenleaf. This steamer was formerly owned by Mr. Albert Davenport of Boston. She was named the Careita, and on her he used to take his many friends to sail from Squirrel Island to the places of interest along the coast. She was then sailed by Capt. Seth Rowe, of Boothbay Harbor.

There are several of these pounds scattered along the coast of Maine. They are artificial ponds of salt water formed by partially damming up small coves to retain tide water sufficient to keep large numbers of lobsters alive for several months. The dealers purchase them when plenty and cheap, and retain them to sell when scarce and high. The capacity of these pounds varies from ten to one hundred fifty thousand each. Capt. A. D. McLain of Pemaquid Beach, and Robert H. Oram, formerly carried on the business of catching small fish, principally herring, in traps, on Johns River, supplying the large fishing schooners of Portland, Gloucester, Boston and other places with bait for their trips to the Georgies Banks and other fishing shoals on our New England coast. Capt. McLain was drowned while engaged in this work by falling from his boat. The canning-factories use many of these small fish, and the cans are sometimes labeled "Sardines," "Brook Trout," etc. Excellent clams are found up this river, and many lobsters are also caught here.

Along the high western ridge, opposite the head-waters of this river, are to be seen the fine dwellings formerly occupied by William Clark and William McClintock, but now by Robert Sproul and William Feeney of Boston. The cleared land of these farms extends to the water's edge. Mr. Clark has pointed out to me many cellars and other excavations, called "pits," along the head-waters of this river, which were used by the first settlers, whose descendants, the Clarks and Drummonds, still reside in town, and the Norths, who now reside in Augusta, Maine, and who often in summer time visit the site of the homes of their ancestors.

Now as the steamer approaches Johns Island, coming straight from the "Thread of Life," we will give further notice to that which attracts our attention :

The many little row and sail boats, now propelled by naphtha, which we have observed all along our course, are those of the lobster-catchers ; their small buoys hold up the lines that lead to their traps at the bottom of the river and ocean. Many people along the coast follow this occupation. As we pass up the east side of this island we see that about one-third of it is covered with trees on the south end, with an open field on the north. It contains in all about eighteen acres, has a fine spring of water under the bank, at the head of a cove, which we pass closely, and which forms a harbor for small boats at high tide. Among its evergreens are the prettiest beds of moss I ever saw. A vein of trap rock, perhaps twenty feet wide divides it, running east and west across the island, where at each end the sea has washed out many cubical fragments, leaving narrow inlets with steep and rugged walls that cannot fail to interest the student of nature who makes a close examination of them when the tide is out. One walled cellar still remains near the little cove, where lived, at different times, Solomon Davis, Ezekiel Thurston and William McLain. Many of the population of Pemaquid Beach to-day are decendants of Mr. McLain. This island was formerly owned by Mr. J. W. Partridge, and was his favorite pasture for sheep, where they could be kept secure without the expense of fencing. A battle between the Indians and English soldiers once took place here, in which twenty-five whites were killed. Crumbling mounds of shells, bones and stone implements found, tell us that the red man once dwelt here. The largest stone tomahawk in possession of the Pemaquid Improvement Association was ploughed up on this island. Of recent years Sabbath-school picnic parties from villages near, with baked and chowdered clams, lobsters, green corn and other refreshments, and with baseball and such games for amusement, have been enjoyed.

Next in line is Beaver Island, with a few spruce trees yet standing. Two more barren ledges between that and the mainland complete the southern out-cropping of this central peninsula spoken of above, which forms the western boundary of Pemaquid Outer Harbor.

Upon the extreme end of this peninsula is located the unique summer home of the noted actress, Mrs. Annie Russell York and her husband. They, with many of their friends, occupy this locality for two or three months each summer, where they are entertained both in doors and out. Their tea house and lawn, beautiful garden of rare flowers and shrubs, salt-water swimming pool and pleasant nooks shaded by the natural growth of evergreen, and with a naphtha launch for pleasure and fishing trips at will, they have ample means for enjoying their summer vacation.

On our right are two more ledges, known as Knowles' Rock and Fish Point, which forms the south and eastern boundary of this fine outer harbor of Pemaquid. This point was formerly occupied by a large porgy factory and other buildings, with an extensive business requiring five or six large steamboats and many men. It is now occupied by the Hotel Waneta, kept by Mrs. Roxanna Varley.

There is little to tell of Beaver Island, except that in recent years it has been used for a summer resort for a few sheep, two at a time being all its scant vegetation would supply with food, and naught but the dew to quench their thirst. In ancient times, as tradition tells, when the Fort was attacked by three French frigates of war, one or more of them sought refuge behind this island to load their cannons, and then, with a cable attached to a kedge, or small anchor, hauled out the frigate, and after discharging a broadside at the fort, retreated to load again.

Crossing Pemaquid Outer Harbor in a northeasterly direction, our steamer makes its landing at Pemaquid Beach. Here we will land and continue our investigation of the history of this once noted place. Pemaquid is noted for what it has been, more than what it is today.

CHAPTER III.

When was Pemaquid First Settled? A Mystery Yet Unsolved.

ONE of the mysteries concerning this place is the *exact date* when the first house was built, the first street laid out, or paved. The first settlers wisely clung to their ships, where they were always at home. No emergency of starvation threatened their extermination, as at Plymouth, for from their fishing grounds beneath them they could at will extract the choicest food to be obtained, ranging from the fine oyster, which was once abundant in this vicinity, but now nearly extinct because the water is colder than formerly, to the "great fat cod." Gradually those who wished to settle on shore cleared away the great pines, spruces, oak and birch, that covered the soil in this vicinity, and erected permanent homes; slowly working back from the rivers, harbors and bays, which were formerly their highways of travel.

On the west bank of the Pemaquid River are three cellars, the first one near the water, where one of the early settlers made his home. Clearing the land around him and extending farther inland, he moved his house to the site where still is to be seen the second cellar, and so on until the third settlement was made near what is now the public highway.

Our history is unlike that of Plymouth and many other places. There was no one here who, like Governor Bradford, kept a journal of passing events on shore; or, if there was, the records may have been destroyed during the many struggles of the three contending nations which captured the place and each for a while held control of it. This being on the eastern outskirts of New England, and claimed as part of Acadia by the French Catholics, was for more than a century the contending ground between them, the Indians, and the English Protestant settlers.

In possession of the author is a copy of a map found among the archives of Spain, of Point Popham, at the mouth of the Kennebec, showing a plan of Fort St. George, which was built there by the Popham Colony in 1607–8. Spain watched with jealous eye the early English settlements here, on what they claimed as their territory. Zuniga, ambassador of King Philip III. of Spain, to England, reported in 1606 the project of Chief Justice Popham, whom he designates as a "great Puritan." On the 5th of March, 1610, Zuniga reports: "I am told vessels are loading at Plymouth (Eng.) with men to people the country they have taken, and that colonies from Exeter and Plymouth are on two large rivers."

In 1613 England, replying to charges of Spain concerning the above recorded settlements, through Carleton, Secretary of State, declared "that she had no possessions in the premises; that England by discovery and actual possession had paramount title, through two colonies, whereof the latter is yet there remaining." This agrees with Captain Smith's account in 1614.

France also has many records of Old Pemaquid, and on their charts, like those of Spain, the territory now called New England was marked New France. A globe three hundred years old, found at Paris, and another at New York, brought from Spain, shows this part of the world marked New France on the former, and New Spain on the latter.

It is not strange that our scholars and historians have failed to obtain the records across the water pertaining to this place, those of France not being accessible to a person with the influence of Hon. J. P. Baxter of Portland, who is President of both the Maine and New England Historical and Genealogical Societies, without a guard to accompany him. Only recently other plans and records have been obtained from French and English documents that will be mentioned in connection with forts erected here. In this country I have found history relating to Old Pemaquid extending from Jamestown, Va., along the sea coast to North Haven, Maine. Only a few threads from each locality can be woven into this sketch as no ordinary volume would contain the detail of all the documents I have fortunately been able to examine during the past twenty years. The fact is, we have not known exactly where to look for the history of Pemaquid, and a vast amount being disguised under some other title, it cannot be readily found. Over thirty books and manuscripts are to be had at the Boston and State Libraries with some history pertaining to Pemaquid.

CHAPTER IV.

Pemaquid As It Was and As It Is.

THE story we have of Pemaquid gives an account of Capt. George Waymouth's visit to this place with his ship, Archangel, and twenty-nine men, in 1605. Having taken a glance at Pemaquid as it appears to-day, as we approach it from the west by water, let us see how it looked to the early voyagers who came here from the east in 1605 and 1607.

Soon after coming to Pemaquid in 1888, I met Mr. William Howard, then stopping with his family at the Jamestown Hotel, who told me of a book in the possession of Mr. Daniel Penniman, of New Harbor, which he kindly presented to me. I was happy to find that it contained much information concerning the early history of Pemaquid which I was in search of. This little book is entitled: "Rosier's Narrative of Waymouth's Voyage to the Coast of Maine in 1605." This interesting narrative was first furnished by Professor Sparks from England in 1843, and abounds with glowing and truthful descriptions of our coast; the manners and customs of the natives, etc. The visits of the Norsemen previously spoken of, the passing fishermen of Spain, France, Portugal and England, who visited these shores, some as early as 1517; the voyage of Bartholomew Gosnold in 1602, and the voyage of Capt. Martin Pring in 1603, are all of general historic interest, but they do not refer to Pemaquid in particular.

Spain and Portugal once claimed all the New World by gift of the Pope of Rome; but England and France refused to acquiesce in this division of the earth's surface. It is said that the king of France, when he heard of the agreement of Spain

Pemaquid Village, looking East from the Masthead of the Schooner W. H. Moody, as She lay in the Outer Harbor

The White Crescent Sand Beach at Pemaquid

and Portugal, pleasantly remarked, "I should be glad to see the claws in Adam's will, which makes that continent their inheritants exclusively." England and France afterwards combined to break the power of Spain, "then the mistress of the seas," and by the destruction of her war fleet, called the Spanish Armada, in 1588, for a time stayed the brutal hand of Spain, which for years had planned the cruel torture and destruction of all those who opposed her. Then those two nations who before had feared to claim this territory, became bitter rivals, and here on this historic ground of Pemaquid, was waged the bitterest warfare of their strife, continuing from the period of their first attempts at settlement on these shores to the close of the French and Indian Wars in 1759. The wily French jesuit and priest secured the service of the natives of old Ma-voo-shen, the Indian name by which most of the territory of this state was first known.

The French were especially active, and in 1603 Henry IV. granted a charter of Acadia, embracing a large part of our territory now known as New England, to DeMonts a Frenchman, who was appointed lieutenant-general of the new territory. He came with his company first to the St. Croix River, fortified on Neutral Island and remained one winter, then removed to Port Royal (now Annapolis, Nova Scotia), and begun a settlement which became so important to the French holdings in America.

The effect of this was to excite the English to new exertions; and in the year of 1605 occured the memorable voyage of Capt. George Waymouth. Capt. Waymouth sailed from England, March 31. Our island of Monhegan was the first land which they saw on reaching this coast. After anchoring their ship at the north of it they landed to obtain supplies of wood and water. They describe it as "wooded, grown with fir, birch, oak and beech. On the verge grew gooseberries, strawberries, wild peas, and wild rose bushes, and much fowl of different kinds bred upon the shore and rocks."

While we were on shore, our men aboard with a few hooks got about 30 (thirty) great cods and haddocks, which gave us a taste of the great plenty of fish, which we found afterward where so ever we went along the coast." Capt. Waymouth then took his ship in toward the mainland and found a good harbor, well protected by several large islands, which have been known in the past as St. George's, but are now called George's Islands. They stopped about these islands until the 16th of June, sounding the depths of the water near them, and exploring a river, which they named Pentecost, now known as George's River, lying directly between George's Islands and the mountains which they described, now called the Blue hills or Camden Mountains. They there built a pinnace or small boat, felled trees, dug a well and sowed peas and barley to test the fertility of the soil.

Wednesday, the 29th of May, they set up a Cross on one of these islands. On the 30th they were visited by Indians from other islands and mainland. These visits were returned by the white people and a pleasant intercourse with much traffic continued until the departure of their ship. He states: "for knives, glasses, combs and other trifles to the value of four or five shillings, we had forty good beaver's skins, otter's skins, sables and other small skins which we knew not how to call." They were earnestly requested to trade with their "Bashaba" or king, and "bring their ship up to his house," but the offer was declined. In a few days they became very friendly and would come on board the ship to eat, seeming much pleased with the food given them. The narrator says, "I noted they would eat nothing raw, neither fish or flesh." They are described as being very witty and ingenious.

"The shape of their body is very proportionable, they are well countenanced, not very tall nor big, but in stature like to us; they paint their bodies with black, their faces, some with red, some with black, and some with blue.

"Their clothing is beaver skins, or deer skins, cast over

Cross on Allen's Island

them like a mantle, and hanging down to their knees, made fast together upon the shoulder with leather; some of them had sleeves, most had none; some had buskins of such leather sewed.

" They suffer no hair to grow on their faces, but on their heads very long and very black, which those who have wives, bind up behind with a leather string, in a long round knot.

" They seemed all very civil and merry, showing tokens of much thankfulness for those things we gave them. We found them there (as after) a people of exceeding good invention, quick understanding and ready capacity.

" Their canoes are made without any iron, of the bark of a birch tree, strengthened within with ribs and hoops of wood, in so good fashion, with such excellent ingenious art, as they are able to bear seven or eight persons, far exceeding any in the Indies.

" This we noted as we went along, they in their canoe with three oars, would at their will go ahead of us and about us when we rowed with eight oars strong; such was their swiftness by reason of the lightness and artificial composition of their canoe and oars."

The women are described as follows:

" Here we saw four of their women, who stood behind them as desirous to see us, but not willing to be seen; for before when so ever we came on shore, they retired into the woods, whether it were in regard of their own natural modesty, being covered, only as the men with the foresaid beaver's skins, or by the commanding jealousy of their husbands, which we rather suspected, because it is an inclination much noted to be in savages; wherefore we would by no means seem to take any special notice of them. They were very well favored in proportion of countenance, though colored black, low of stature, and fat, bareheaded as the men, wearing their hair long; they had two little male children of a year and a half old as we judged, very fat and of good countenance, which they love tenderly, all naked except their legs, with which covered with their leather buskin sewed, fastened with straps to a girdle about their waist, which they gird very straight, and is decked round about with little round pieces of red copper; to these I gave chains, and bracelets, glasses, and other trifles, which the savages seemed to accept with great kindness."

In reference to the five Pemaquid Indians captured on this voyage, the narrator says:

"Further I have thought fit to add some things worthy to be regarded, which we have observed from the savages since we took them. First although at the time when we surprised them, they made their best resistance, not knowing our purpose, nor what we were, nor how we meant to use them; yet after perceiving by their kind usage we intend them no harm, they have never since seemed discontented with us, but very tractable, loving and willing by their best means to satisfy us in anything we demand of them, by words or signs for their understanding; neither have they at any time been at the least discord among themselves; insomuch as we have not seen them angry, but merry; and so kind, as if you give anything to one of them, he will distribute part to everyone of the rest. We have brought them to understand some English, and we understand much of their language; so we are able to ask them many things. And this we have observed, that if we show them anything, and ask them if they have it in their country, they will tell you if they have, and the use of it, the difference from ours in bigness, color, or form; but if they have it not, be it a thing never so precious, they will deny the knowledge of it.

"They have names for many stars which they will show in the firmament.

"They show great reverence to their king, and are in great subjection to their governors, and they will show a great respect to any we tell them are our commanders.

"They show the manner of how they make bread of their

Waymouth and His Company, as Represented at Allen's Island, July 6, 1905

Indian wheat, and how they make butter and cheese of the milk they have of the reindeer and fallow deer, which they have tame as we have cows.

"They have excellent colors. And having seen our indigo, they make show of it, or of some other like thing which maketh as good a blue.

"One special thing is their manner of killing the whale, which they call Pow-da-we; and will describe his form; how he bloweth up the water; and that he is twelve fathoms long; and that they go in company of their king with a multitude of their boats, and strike him with a bone made in fashion of a harping iron fastened to a rope, which they made great and strong of the bark of trees, which they veer out after him; then all their boats come about him, and as he riseth above water, with their arrows they shoot him to death; when they have killed him and dragged him to shore, they call all their chief lords together, and sing a song of joy; and those chief lords whom they call sagamores, divide the spoil, and give to every man a share, which pieces so distributed, they hang up about their houses for provisions; and when they boil them, they blow off the fat, and put to their peas, maize, and other pulse which they eat."

In referring to the abundance of fish and their manner of catching them, he writes:

"We drew with a small net of twenty fathoms very nigh the shore; we got about thirty very good and great lobsters, many rock fish, some plaice and other small fishes, and fishes called lumps, very pleasant to the taste; and we generally observed, that all the fish, of what kind so ever we took, were well fed, fat, and sweet in taste.

"All along the shore, and some space within, where the wood hindereth not, grow plentifully, raspberries, gooseberries, strawberries, roses, currants, wild vines, angelica.

"Within the island grow wood of sundry sorts, some very great, and all tall, as birch, beech, ash, maple, spruce, cherry tree, yew, oak, very great and good, fir tree, out of which issueth turpentine in so marvelous plenty, and so sweet, as our chirurgeon (Physician) and others affirmed they never saw so good in England. We pulled off much gum, congealed on the outside of the bark, which smelled like frankincense. This would be a great benefit for making tar and pitch."

The capture of five Pemaquid Indians with two canoes, with all their bows and arrows, was an event of the uttermost importance on this voyage. The kidnapping of these Indians seemed an act of vandalism unworthy of men who professed to be Christians, as they did. Rosier claims that the capture was for the benefit of both nations, that on learning the language of each other, it would be a "public good and zeal of promulgating God's holy church, by planting Christianity, to be the sole intent of the honorable setters forth of this discovery."

The first account of this voyage published in England on their return, together with the five Indian captives, Nahanada, sagamore or commander; Amoret, Skicowaros, Maneddo, gentlemen; Saffacomoit, a servant; created widespread interest in that country. On his return, Capt. Waymouth first landed at Plymouth, England, where Sir Ferdinando Gorges was then captain; and he was so much interested in the Indians that he took three of them into his own family. Many years afterwards, when writing his "Brief Narration" of his efforts to colonize New England, he says: "This accident must be acknowledged the means under God of putting a foot and giving life to all our plantations."

The account of Waymouth's voyage, as first published, has puzzled those historians who depended upon that alone, because the longitude of the locality and the course of the river and mountains from their ship, while at anchor at Pentecost Harbor, were purposely omited to prevent their rivals from learning of the precise locality of their discovery. Now all doubt has been set at rest by the publication of that information which was kept at the time by Capt. Waymouth's

Memorial of Waymouth's Voyage, 1605

log-book, so that now it has been proven that Monhegan Island (then called St. George) was the first island discovered and landed upon; George's Islands (afterward named St. George's by the Popham Colony in 1607) the first harbor entered, where the Cross was set up; George's River leading up to Thomaston, the first river entered; the Camden Mountains, the ones which the voyagers "had constantly in view." Another Cross was erected 12 miles up the river at Thomaston. These were to establish the claim of the English people to this territory as the discoverers in 1605. The celebration of the three hundredth anniversary of Capt. George Waymouth's voyage to the coast of Maine in 1605, was observed on July 6th, 1905, at St. George's Island and at Thomaston by the Maine Historical Society, assisted by the government revenue cutter Woodbury from Portland, and the United States monitor Arkansas.

A stone cross was erected on the island with proper inscription, and one of wood at Thomaston; there also a large boulder was set up on the common, bearing a bronze tablet. Interesting services were held at the island at the unveiling of the cross, participated in by visitors from the government steamers, the Bristol from Pemaquid, the Castine and G. W. Butman from Rockland, with sail and row boats, with many people from east and west.

Prayer was offered by Rev. C. E. Gould, an address of much historical interest was given by Mr. George Arthur Smith. At the conclusion of the exercises on Allen's island, the visitors from the Woodbury returned to the cutter, where an elegant lunch was served by the General Knox Chapter, D. A. R. At the close of the lunch the Woodbury, Arkansas, and a large fleet of smaller crafts proceeded up the river. The sail up the river (the St. George's) of Waymouth's discovery was delightful, being marked by frequent salutes fired by interested parties at different points along the shore. An interesting feature of this trip was a boat loaded with some fifteen people, dressed to represent the early English mariners, as they appeared when sailing up this river three hundred years ago, with Dr. W. J. Jameson of Thomaston as Capt. Waymouth and three Indians for pilots.

At Thomaston a salute was fired from the Woodbury in honor of Governor Cobb. A procession was then formed on shore headed by Waymouth's crew, the Indians and about one hundred and twenty-five school children, with the Camden Cornet Band at the head. At the Mall about two thousand people had assembled to witness the exercises connected with the unveiling of the memorial erected by the town. Hon. Joseph E. Moore presided, and gave the address of welcome. The invocation was given by Rev. W. A. Newcomb D. D. of Thomaston.

He was followed by other speakers, Hon. James P. Baxter, President of the Maine Historical and New England Historic Genealogical Societies, and Hon. Willian T. Cobb, Governor of Maine. At the close of the addresses, the memorial tablet was unveiled by Miss Ruth Flint Linnell of Thomaston. The tablet bears the following inscription:—

To Commemorate the Voyage of
Captain
George Waymouth
To the Coast of Maine
in 1605
His Discovery and Exploration of the
St. George's River
And Planting a Cross on the
Northerly Shore of this Harbor
Where the River "Trended Westward"
The Earliest Known Claim of
Right of Possession by Englishmen
On New England Soil
This Tablet is Erected by the
Town of Thomaston
1905.

Mr. J. B. Keating, British Vice Consul at Portland then

Hon. John B. Keating, British Vice Consul at Portland

delivered an address and was followed by General Joshua L. Chamberlain. The closing address being made by Hon. Charles E. Littlefield of Rockland. Music by the band and singing by the children added to the interest of the occasion. Refreshments were served in a public hall during the afternoon, and the historical program continued by addresses in the evening by Mr. Baxter and Dr. Burrage, at Watts' Hall, which was prettily decorated with English and American flags and evergreens. The exercises closed there by the rendering of a delightful solo by Mrs. Ernestine Fish of Boston, and a poem, entitled " Westward to England," by Miss Rita Creighton Smith of Thomaston.

All of these addresses, with an account of the celebration, fill a pamphlet of over fifty pages, which can be found in the Portland library, entitled Waymouth Tercentenary. I deem the following note found on page 35, which contains a part of Mr. Baxter's address, exceedingly interesting to investigators of our history:

"Capt. George Waymouth had been supposed to be a rough old mariner until I discovered some years ago, in what is known as the King's Library in the British Museum, a manuscript volume by him entitled the " Jewel of Artes " which he presented to King James I. not long before his voyage to Maine. This volume had remained nearly three centuries unnoticed, and I had it reproduced and bound precisely like the original volume. A glance at it will show that the author was an educated man and well versed in the science of his time."

This brief account of that celebration should not be closed without reference to the spirit of good will and kindness, and the deep interest every one seemed to take in the whole proceedings, by the display of English and American flags and other emblems with which they decorated their places of business and private residences.

A delightful informal reception was given in their Thomaston homes, especially by Dr. and Mrs. J. E. Walker at their beautiful colonial home. The spacious rooms, fragrant with the scent of innumerable roses and pinks, and bright with English and American flags, the brilliant uniforms of the naval officers mingling with the lighter colors of the dresses of the ladies, presented a picture long to be remembered with pleasure.

It is well not to forget the friendly natives of this locality which three centuries ago occupied this land, with the wild game then abundant, when great forests covered the shores, which caused Capt. John Smith who visited here in 1614, to exclaim "I wonder how so great trees can grow on the Islands and main of this country." Now this fair land is nearly covered with the verdant vegetation planted by the white man, and the race that met them so long ago, and lived in peace with them for more than fifty years, have passed beyond.

Hon. James P. Baxter

CHAPTER V.

An Account of the Historical Celebration at the Mouth of the Kennebec River in 1907

AS a result of that " glowing narrative " of Waymouth's voyage to the coast of Maine, with the exhibition of the Indians brought from there, was the chartering of the company for colonizing America called the Council of Virginia. The charter authorized the formation of two companies, called the London and Plymouth companies, the latter being the only one which will concern us, being authorized to settle this part of the country which was then known as North Virginia.

During the year of 1606, the Lord Chief Justice of England Sir John Popham, and several other gentlemen deeply interested in the discoveries already made on this coast, sent two vessels to attempt further discoveries. The one in which Sir John Popham was interested, was captured by the Spanish. But the spring of 1607 opened with new and better prospects. The settlement of Jamestown, Va., was begun by the London company. The Popham colony then made an attempt, under the auspices of the Plymouth company, to found a plantation at the mouth of the Kennebec river, then called the Sagadahoc. This expedition sailed from Plymouth, June 10th, 1607, in two ships, the larger one called the " Mary and John," and the smaller one called a fly boat, named the " Gift of God." Beside their crews they had " one hundred and twenty persons for planters." Comparing this with the Jamestown, Va., colony on the Newport, May, 1607, of one hundred and five passengers, and the Mayflower of December

20, 1620, with one hundred and two Pilgrims, we note that the Pemaquid colony was the largest both in number of ships and people. They left Plymouth, Eng., on the last day of May and sighted Monhegan on the 6th of August, and found anchorage by the George's islands, probably agreed on as their place of rendezvous before leaving England. On the following day they sought a more secure harbor, doubtless that of Capt. Waymouth, because they found the Cross he set up, and at once made preparations for an excursion westward to the Pemaquid river.

The words of the narrator best tell the story:

" About midnight Capt. Gilbert caused his shipp's boat to be mannde with fourteen persons and the Indian Skidwares (brought to England by Capt. Weymouth,) and rowed to the westward from their ship, to the river of Pemaquid, which they found to be four leagues distant from the shipp where she rode. The Indian brought them to the salvages' houses, where they found a hundred men, women and children, and their commander, or sagamore, among them, named Nahanada, who had been brought likewise into England by Capt. Waymouth, and returned thither by Capt. Hanham, setting forth for those parts and some part of Canada the year before; at their first coming the Indians betooke them to their armes, their bowes and arrowes; but after Nahanada had talked with Skidwares and perceaved that they were English men, he caused them to lay aside their bowes and arrowes, and he himself came unto them and ymbraced, and made them much welcome, and entertayned them with much chierfulness, and did they likewise him, and after two howers thus interchangeably spent, they returned abourd again.

Sunday 9th, the chief of both the shipps, with the greatest part of all the company, landed on the island where the crosse stood, the which they called St. George's Island, and heard a sermon delivered unto them by Mr. Seymour, his preacher, and soe returned abourd againe.

Site of Old Fort and House at Beginning of Excavation of the Front Wall. Edgemere and Bayview Houses in the Distance, Across the Outer and Inner Harbors, at the Mouth of the Pemaquid River

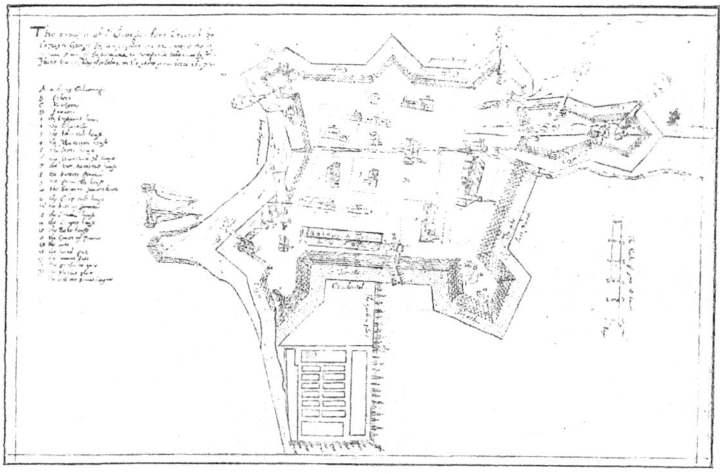

Important Plan of Fort Popham, Built at the Mouth of the Kennebec River in 1607-8, by the English Colony which First Landed at Pemaquid

Monday 10th, Capt. Popham manned his shallop, and Capt. Gilbert his boat, with fifty persons in both, and departed for the river of Pemaquid, carrieing with them Skidwares, and arrived in the mouthe of the river: there came forth Nahanada, with all his company of Indians, with their bowes and arrowes in their handes. They, being before his dwelling house, would willingly have all our people come ashore, using them all in kind sort after their manner; nevertheless, after one hower they all suddenly withdrew themselves into the woodes, nor was Skidwares desirous to return with them any more aboard. Our people loth to proffer any violence into them by drawing him by force, suffered him to stay behind, promising to return to them the day following, but he did not. After his departure they imbarked themselves and rowed to the further side of the river, and there remayned on shoare for the night.

They returned to their shipps toward the evening, where they still road under St. George Island.

They weyed anchors and sett saile to goe for the river of Sachadehoc; they had little wynd and kept their course west."

The extract from Strachey is of deep interest to us as we learn that one at least, of the Indians, seized by Waymouth two years previous, was a Sagamore of Old Pemaquid. He is called Nahanada, Tahanedo, and Dehaneda—which are only different ways of spelling the same name. His character as chief whenever brought before us, appears to good advantage. After residing in England about a year he returned in 1606. His kind reception, with that of his subjects, to the Popham colony, was quite in contrast with his treatment by Capt. Waymouth. We next hear of Nahanada October 3d, when he makes his appearance again at the settlement at the mouth of the Kennebec, attended by his wife, and having in company a brother of the bashaba, Amenquin, another Sagamore, and his ever faithful attendant, Skidwares. This time they remained some three days, one of them being the Sabbath. Being invited by the president, they attended public worship, behaving in all respects with the most perfect propriety. At their departure, Popham, president of the colony, bestowed upon them some trifling presents, promising to visit in person the bashaba at Penobscot, and make arrangements for a regular trade.

From the " Tercentenery " of the landing of the Popham Colony, we learn of a meeting held there to celebrate the event, on Aug. 29th, 1907. An address was given by Mr. James P. Baxter at that time, when much valuable information was obtained pertaining to this colony. On another page is a cut showing the site of the Fort and a plan of it, on which a Tablet has been erected to commemorate the event with the following inscription upon it:

THE FIRST ENGLISH COLONY,
ON THE SHORES OF NEW ENGLAND
WAS FOUNDED HERE
AUGUST 29 N. S. 1607
UNDER
GEORGE POPHAM

This fort was called St. George's.

The First Colony of the French on the New England shores was established by de Monts in 1604 east of the Penobscot river. This plan here shown of the Fort was found at Simancos, Spain, by the Hon. J. L. M. Curry, United States Minister to Spain, in recent years. This was the beginning of English occupancy of New England, although not permanent. The beginning of ship building on the American coast by the construction of the ship Virginia. The beginning of self Government in the colonies, and it must have the respect which as Emerson says, " Always belongs to first things."

CHAPTER VI.

THE VOYAGE OF CAPT. JOHN SMITH OF POCAHONTAS FAME.

AFTER making a permanent settlement at Jamestown, Va., Smith was injured by an explosion of gun-powder in 1609, and returned to England for surgical aid. He was appointed Admiral of New England, and in 1614 with a small boat and eight men surveyed the New England coast from the mouth of the Penobscot River to Cape Cod, including our bay of Pemaquid and the harbor of Plymouth. He named New England in honor of Old England, Cape Ann, Charles River and Cape Elizabeth, which still retain the names he gave them. By request of Smith, Prince Charles of England, afterwards Charles I., named Pemaquid, St. John's town, and Monhegan, Batties Island.

Smith had under his command a ship and bark with forty-five men. They came here "to take whales, and make trials of a mine of gold and copper; they were not successful in either enterprise, but they secured a good quantity of codfish, and for a small sum purchased a large amount of furs of the Indians." Smith says, while his ships lay at Monhegan, "right against him in the main was a ship of Sir Francis Popham," and "forty leagues to the westward were two French ships, that had made then a great voyage by trade." This shows that at that period there was considerable intercourse between Europe and our Maine seacoast.

Smith tells of a ship seen at New Harbor sent out by Sir Francis, son of George Popham, president of the colony, in command of Capt. Williams, and it is claimed this ship indicates the English were maintaining control of the territory.

Some have said there are no good Indians, but I am proud of the record of ours of old Pemaquid. Capt. Smith again bears testimony to the good character of our Indian chief Nahanada and his friends, whom he affirms kindly assisted him whenever he desired them to. Smith says: "The main assistance next God I had to this small number was my acquaintance among the salvadges, especially with Dohannida, (Nahanada) one of their greatest lords who had lived long in England."

I submit the following for defence of Capt. Smith whose veracity for truth has been questioned by some historians within a few years past. The truth of the story of Pocahontas and Smith was never doubted till 1866, when the eminent antiquary, Dr. Charles Dean of Cambridge, in reprinting Smith's books, found that he had not spoken of it in his first book, which was published about 1618. John Clark Ridpath, author of one of our best histories of the United States says of Capt. Smith—"His was a strange and wonderful career! John Smith was altogether the most noted man in the early history of America. There is no reason in the world for doubting the truth of this affecting and romantic story; one of the most marvelous and touching in the history of any nation." I have read many favorable accounts of Smith written by his contemporaries; will simply quote one by Thomas Carlton.

"I never knew a warrior yet, but thee,
From wine, tobacco, dice, debts and oaths so free."

Among the early charts of five different nations: the English, French, Spanish, Portugese and Dutch, who were in early times struggling for a foothold upon this continent, I find upon examination, that of Capt. John Smith is far superior to that of any other. Smith's description of this part of the country, and the publication of his map of the coast, was an important event in our history.

CHAPTER VII.

EARLY TRAFFIC AT PEMAQUID.

CONSIDERABLE business was transacted along this coast with the fisheries and fur trade, which centered chiefly at Monhegan and Pemaquid, as we have evidence by the records of the number of ships sailing here annually from Europe. It has been determined that between the years 1607 and 1622, no less than " 109 ships entered and cleared from the harbors of Pemaquid and its dependencies, where they did more or less business in the discharge and receipt of cargoes and commerce with Europe." The English ships employed in transporting emigrants to Virginia with their necessary supplies, found it for their interest, on their return, to call on this coast and obtain such return cargoes of fish and furs as the constantly increasing business of the country was able to afford.

" While the Pilgrims were struggling for life at Plymouth, and Conant was founding Cape Ann," says Thornton, "Pemaquid was probably the busiest place on the coast." J. Wingate Thornton of Massachusetts, was a reliable historian, and another quotation of his is worthy to be mentioned, which reads as follows: " To Pemaquid we must look for the initiation of civilization into New England."

Smith says, that the ship of Sir Francis Popham had been accustomed to trade at the port of New Harbor several years previously, that is to 1614. The definite lines of an old fort with foundation walls 51 x 52 feet square, and 5 feet thick, were to be seen till recently. This fort was located about 3 rods south of the Tablet set up on land of C. B. Meserve to commemorate the first deed published in America. The stone foundations were removed in 1913. Many cellars can still be traced about New Harbor. Choice relics have been found in that vicinity; the fragments of ancient mill-stones, unglazed earthen pottery, remains of kettles, large spoons, lead, bullets in large quantities, a leaden relic of trade, such as was used by the English people in olden times to tag cloth with, with the date of 1610 upon it.

In 1622 there were thirty ships trading and fishing about Pemaquid; that no doubt included Boothbay Harbor, Damariscove, Monhegan, New Harbor and Pemaquid as known to-day. One gentleman has suggested that Pemaquid was not entitled to the credit of this number of ships, and suggested that they must have belonged to Damariscove, but he could not have been familiar with that place, for as one fisherman aptly remarked: "there is not room to moor thirty dories in that harbor, let alone thirty ships," all of which must have been large enough to cross the ocean. The harbor of Monhegan is not more suitable for that number of ships, neither is New Harbor. I find a statement sworn to by Abraham Shurte, stating that "Damariscove with all the islands adjacent belonged to Pemaquid;" twenty or more. Another reason why this which is known as Pemaquid Beach must have been the principal resort for fishing and trading is on account of its excellent harbors, and being by far the best locality for the fishermen to obtain bait which they found in great abundance at the Falls of the Pemaquid River which have ever since supplied bait for the fishermen and excellent food for the people of this locality, known as "smoked alewives." These fish come here from the southern waters every spring like the migratory birds. To this day many of the large fishermen which sail from Boston, Gloucester and Portland, visit this place to obtain fresh bait; the alewives of the Pemaquid River are especially sought for during their season, being considered the best bait that can be obtained to catch halibut.

From the following copied account and other writings of

early times, some have been led to think that Damariscove and Monhegan were superior to Pemaquid, but the testimony of Shurte teaches us differently. It was natural that the early mariners should write of these islands as they did, they being the most conspicuous to them when they approached or passed this locality in their ships. No one familiar with this whole region can for a moment doubt that this was the metropolis of this locality, as stated in history. Even to-day, after centuries have elapsed, during which man and nature have combined to lay waste and obliterate the remains of its former civilization, there is more left beneath the waters of its harbors, along the banks of its noted river, its waterfalls and its tributary lakes for twenty miles back into the country, and in much of the territory then known as the "kingdom of Pemaquid;" more relics of early civilization yet remain here than can be found at Plymouth and Jamestown, Virginia, combined. The Pemaquid River was once noted for its wild game; its waters were the highways of the natives leading back to the territory where they trapped and shot wild game and procured the fine furs which foreign ships came here to purchase.

"Among the scattered specks of struggling civilization, dotting the skirts of the green primeval forests," said Adams, "the little colony of Plymouth was not the least." This little colony had been established only about eighteen months. It had struggled through its second winter, and now, sadly reduced in number, with supplies wholly exhausted, the Pilgrims were sorely distressed. They were entirely destitute of bread. There was an emergency of starvation at Plymouth. The whole settlement was alive with excitement, when suddenly a boat was seen to cross the mouth of Plymouth Bay and disappeared behind the next headland. A shot was fired as a signal, in answer to which the boat changed course and headed for the harbor. It proved to be the shallop of the Sparrow, Weston's ship, from the Pemaquid dependency of Damariscove, with seven men and a letter from Capt. Hudson, which informed the Pilgrims of the Eastern port, a place of bread and resources of trade. The Waif had sailed forty leagues from places in the eastern parts, known as Monhegan and " Damerill's Isles " (Damariscove) where were many ships. The little boat landed under a salute of three volleys of musketry from the Pilgrims on learning the good news from these "Eastern parts," and its neighborhood.

With the return of the Sparrow's boat, Gov. Bradford sent Winslow, (The author of this book has recently ascertained that he is a descendant of Kanelm Winslow. My great grandmother being named Phebe Winslow, a descendant of those who settled at Plymouth,) with the Pilgrims' shallop and means to purchase food supplies, and piloted back the Pilgrims who first learned the way and the resources of Maine by this waif of her seacoast, where fleets from Bristol and London now crowded the fishing and fur stations of Pemaquid. Thus informed, the hungry Pilgrims eagerly sought for supplies there to be had, and from the ships a " good quantity of provisions were obtained without money and without price, ample to give each Pilgrim a quarter of a pound of bread day by day, till next harvest." " On returning and reporting, the Pilgrims at once prepared to share the profits of the business enterprises at and about Pemaquid, and a fishing vessel was procured, fitted out at Plymouth, and sent into the fisheries there." She reached Boothbay Harbor and sought the anchorage, where ships from England used to ride. In 1624, many English ships were there. A terrible storm came on which drove the Plymouth ship ashore, a wreck, when she sunk, the captain and one man being lost. By help there obtained, the wrecked vessel was raised and floated by casks attached to the keel at low water, taken ashore and repaired, refitted and put again into Pilgrim service.

I have found that some people who have visited this place, though apparently well posted in history, are not willing to admit the former importance of old Pemaquid. That may be excusable from visitors from Massachusetts who have forgotten, or never knew that during much of the period of its most striking events, this place was as much in Massachusetts as ancient Plymouth. But the apathy of some of the people of our state is surprising, and I sometimes think that a majority of our best informed citizens have emigrated to other states.

I blame no one for lauding Plymouth and its noble Pilgrim settlers. None too many monuments have been erected, none too many relics preserved, none too much history recorded, all are good and excellent educators, and it is right that our citizens should know as much at least about our own country, as of Africa or Australia. It is plainly shown by the above records that the early settlers of these two colonies must have become mutual friends; like two people from the same town, meeting in foreign ports or cities, they at once became interested in each other's welfare.

Now, what I have to complain of is, that we have but one monument here, and that many of our relics and much of our history have been scattered far and wide, to our disgrace. It has been said, not a monument or tablet has been erected to teach our children, our citizens or our visitors the place where "Civilization began in New England." Where the Pilgrims were presented with the "staff of life" that saved them to our country, where lived and died the noble Indian Samoset who first welcomed them to these New England shores and who saved them "from destruction both by their enemies and from starvation," as they themselves record.

Instead of building up monumental records for education, we have allowed the destruction of many of the choicest ones we had by vandalism and neglect, as the beautiful and elegant mansion, the home of Gen. Henry Knox, once Gen. Washington's trusted friend, Fort Frederick, Fort Farley and many other noted landmarks of the past. Only one of the many forts once scattered along our coast, is left, Fort Edgecomb, a blockhouse near Wiscasset, and in respect to that, the timely interest of a local editor, Mr. Wood, set on foot repairs to which summer visitors contributed, by which it was saved from disgrace and destruction.

Some have spoken with contempt of this place, judging from its present appearance that it could only have been a little "fishing station" in the past. But its fish, even, are not to be sneered at, for they have ever been noted since Waymouth's voyage in 1605. For many generations in the State House at Boston, has hung an effigy of the sacred cod-fish, and when it was transferred from the Old Capital to its new quarters, a few years ago, that august body of legislators on Beacon Hill suspended all other business, while a party of their colleagues bore that sacred emblem of an occupation that helped to build up their city, in state upon a tablet draped with the stars and stripes, carried upon their shoulders and deposited, where it is still to remain in sight of their lawmakers, a reminder of the foundation industries of their commonwealth. Fish and beans, the products of the sea and land, should never be sneered at by those who love the great "Hub of the Universe."

It is on record that from the Pemaquid locality came the food that kept alive that remnant of the Pilgrim band at Plymouth, when starvation stared them in the face that winter and spring of 1622, when their provisions were all gone and no harvest could be had for months. Bradford in his Journal mentions this deliverance. He does not mention Pemaquid specially, but others state that Hudson, the captain who sent the supplies, was at Pemaquid. Should not honorable mention be made of a place which saved to the world a colony which has exerted such untold power for good? The intercourse thus established between this, the earliest surviving settlement and Plymouth, proved also very advantageous to the latter in opening the way for a profitable business for them in these localities, an account of which is on record.

These few bits of history are evidence of the gradual growth of Pemaquid, and the beginning of its recognition as the metropolis of these Eastern shores, a position it held for some years.

" Persevering when others grew weary and retired, Gorges had made a trading station at Pemaquid, the center of the wonderful spring and winter fishery, in that charmed quadrant included between Cape Newagen and Damarels Cove Islands on the west and Monhegan and St. Georges. Thither annually the Virginian and English fishermen came in armed vessels, with crews of forty men to a vessel, forming, as their vessels yearly increased in numbers, a barrier against the westward progress of French settlements.

The stand taken from 1607 to 1620 and onward by these men of Gorges on the mainland and the fishermen on the adjacent islands, was the definite initial of the subsequent dominion of the English-speaking race in America. When they began there were no English settlers nearer than Virginia, but under the lee of these brave fishermen holding the front with fifty or sixty armed ships, settlers did set down on the New England coast, and colonies grew up whose history we trace with filial pride."

CHAPTER VIII.

First Deed Ever Properly Executed In America.

OVER a half-century before William Penn, the noted Friend or Quaker, made his memorable treaty with the Indians, and purchased of them honorably the state of Pennsylvania, John Brown of this place set the example by an honorable purchase of a large tract of land of the original owners at Pemaquid.

Representatives of those two noted names, Smith and Brown, did not fail to appear at Old Pemaquid and are to be found here yet. We have taken note of what Capt. John Smith has accomplished, now we will see what was done by John Brown. The purchase of land of the Pemaquid Indians constitutes another important epoch in our history. Prof. John Johnston's history of Bristol and Bremen states that Brown probably came here direct from Bristol, England, and he copies a document from the records of that place relating to him, dated Feb. 21, 1658, when Robert Allen testified that he had often told him that " he was the son of Richard Brown of Barton Regis, in Gloucester, in England, and that he married Margaret, daughter of Francis Hayward of Bristol."

FIRST DEED EVER PROPERLY EXECUTED IN AMERICA.

In 1625 was given the first deed of land made and acknowledged in New England, perhaps in America, conveying a large tract to one John Brown of New Harbor, at Pemaquid. This deed was signed by Samoset (the same who welcomed the Pilgrims at Plymouth) and Unongoit, two Indian Sagamores.

The affidavit of these two Indians to their deed given for this land is interesting. It reads as follows:—

> To All People Whom it May Concern. Know ye, that I, Capt. John Samoset and Unongoit, Indian sagamores, they being the proper heirs to all the lands on both sides of Muscongus river, have bargained and sold to John Brown of New Harbour this certain tract or parcell of land as followeth, that is to say, beginning at Pemaquid Falls and so running a direct course to the head of New Harbor, from thence to the south end of Muscongus Island, taking in the island, and so running five and twenty miles into the country north and by east, and thence eight miles northwest and by west, and then turning and running south and by west to Pemaquid, where first begun. To all which lands above bounded, the said Capt. John Samoset and Unongoit, Indian sagamores, have granted and made over to the above said John Brown, New Harbour, in and for consideration of fifty skins, to us in hand paid, to our full satisfaction, for the above mentioned lands, and we the above said sagamores do bind ourselves and our heirs forever to defend the above said John Brown and his heirs in the quiet and peaceable possession of the above said lands. In witness whereunto, the said Capt. John Samoset and Unongoit have set our hands and seal this fifteenth day of July, in the year of our Lord God one thousand six hundred and twenty-five.
>
> Capt. John Samoset, (seal)
> Unongoit (seal)
>
> Signed and sealed in presence of us, Matthew Newman.
> Wm. Cox.

> "July 24, 1626. Capt. John Samoset and Unongoit, Indian Sagamores, personally appeared and acknowledged this instrument to be their act and deed, at Pemaquid, before me,
>
> Abraham Shurte."

And the record of its registry is as follows:

> "Charlestown, Dec. 26, 1720. Read, and at the request of James Stilson, and his sister, Margaret Hilton, formally Stilson, they being claimers and heirs of said lands, accordingly entered. Per Samuel Phipps."
>
> One of the clerks of the Committee for Eastern Lands.

I have procured a copy of the above deed with the affidavit concerning its record, which occured nearly one hundred years after the deed was executed, which we have framed and hung up on exhibition in the Castle at Pemaquid.

We know nothing now of Matthew Newman's history, one of the witnesses of this deed, but Johnson says Cox became a resident of this place and his posterity of the name are still here. The late Capt. Israel Cox of Bristol who was one of the selectmen of the town of Bristol, claimed that this William Cox was his great grandfather's father. An interesting circumstance in connection with this deed is that the following list of names, written by the last signer of it, are on our Register, Aug. 28, 1896. 1. William Cox, witness of the first deed executed in America. 2. John of Pemaquid and Sagadahoc. 3. John, Jr. of Sagadahoc and Dorchester. 4. Ebenezer of Dorchester. 5. Benjiman of Hardunk. 6. Benjiman of Vermont. 7. Allen of Vermont. 8. Gardener Cox, M. D., Holyoke, Mass.

The last signer of the above list came here to gather information about his ancestors and to locate land once owned here by them. I think he has since published a history of the family.

In 1897 Mr. Edward J. Cox of Newtonville, Mass., visited this place for the same purpose as the doctor above mentioned and recorded his ancestors' names in an unbroken line of descent to the signer of that deed, he being of the ninth generation.

The precision and conciseness of this deed of conveyance of American soil, written at Pemaquid, and the neat and compact formula of acknowledgment, drawn up by Abraham Shurte, and still adhered to in New England, word for word, are interesting to the jurist. There was no precedent for the acknowledgment, or the formula, and Mr. Shurte is well entitled to be remembered as the father of American conveyancing.

The following witty dedication of his book by the late N. I. Bowditch, Esq., of Boston, in his work on Suffolk Surnames is interesting. "To the memory of Abraham Shurte, the father of American Conveyancing, whose name is associated alike with my daily toilet and my daily occupation.— N. I. BOWDITCH." The first legislation of Massachusetts providing for this mode of authenticating deeds, did not occur until 1640, when commissioners were especially appointed for the purpose, and Plymouth colony did not adopt this security against fraudulent conveyances until six years later, in 1646.

This deed was not recorded for nearly a hundred years, and was then entered on the records at Charlestown, Mass.

I have also a copy of a deed showing that the Plymouth people purchased a large tract of land lying on the Kennebec River, which was deeded to them by our Nahanada and his brother and father. The land in this region being so fertile compared with that of Cape Cod, and the waters so abounding in superior food supplies, the colonists of Plymouth and vicinity come for a share of the bountiful products of Pemaquid.

This citizen of Pemaquid, Abraham Shurte, (sometimes written Shurd, occasionally Short) deserves more than a passing notice, for I wish to show that with the other important relations of Old Pemaquid we had as many good people, both Indians and whites, as any other settlements on the New England coast. Shurte became a resident of Pemaquid soon after his arrival in this country, and spent the rest of his life here. He was active in business and extended his trade along the shore west to Boston and east to Nova Scotia. In one of his excursions when on his way to Boston with Capt. Wright, he came near losing his life by the recklessness of a seaman who, in attempting to light his pipe near a keg of gunpowder, exploded it and blew the vessel and himself to atoms. Shurte and the others escaped. He is always spoken of as a magistrate of influence in the colony. The Indians he always treated kindly and justly, and thus retained their friendship even when they were enraged at others.

In the summer of 1631 near a hundred of the Eastern Indians with thirty canoes, went to Agawam, (now Ipswich, Mass.) killed and captured Indians residing there, among them the wife of one of their Sagamores. Through the influence of Shurte she was restored to the Chief. This probably laid the foundation of the friendship ever afterwards shown him. We have never found the name since in history, and have no reliable record of his death, but learn that in 1662 he was eighty years of age.

Another citizen of Pemaquid is worthy of note, John Earthy, and also Richard Oliver of Monhegan, who deserve praise for their efforts to pacify the Indians, when they threatened danger to the white people. John Earthy was licensed to keep a house of " publicke entertaynmente " at Pemaquid by the Commissioners Court. After visiting Boston in winter time in the interests of this place he returned, and found a vessel lurking on this coast, waiting to capture Indians for slaves, as had been done occasionally for many years. Mr. Earthy hastened to visit the captain and argued with him against doing such injustice to a people with whom they were at peace. He also cautioned the Indians to be on their guard. So the slaver was unsuccessful here, but gained his object farther eastward. His name is mentioned as attending a conference at the Kennebec, to secure peace between the whites and Indians. At this conference were Assiminasqua; chief of the Penobscots, and Madockawando, his adopted son, Tarumkin, a chief of the Androscoggins, Hopegood and Mugg, and many others. Mugg belonged to the Penobscot tribe. The Indians, plainly showing that they had been ill-treated by the whites, seemed to have the best of the argument at this conference. Later we find his name with Oliver's and Isaac Addington's, a well known gentleman of Boston and member of the first church there in 1679, as witnesses to a treaty of peace with the Indians signed by Mugg in behalf of Madockawando and other chiefs at Boston, Nov. 13, 1676.

CHAPTER IX.

NOTED INDIANS—SAMOSSET, UNNONGOIT, NAHANADA.

HERE, at Old Pemaquid we find Indian names of individuals which stand higher on the pinnacle of fame than any others ever yet placed on record for their good and excellent traits of character. The name of the tribe located in this place of whom Nahanada was the chief, was the Wa-wen-ock. We are again bothered by a lack of phonetic spelling which ought to have been adopted long ago. By following our previous rule of placing the accent on the second syllable; we have Sam-os-set, Un-on-go-it, etc.

Unfortunately we have but little history of the early Basha-ba, Unnongoit, Madockawando and others; so of many of the early white settlers connected with this place our records so far are but meagre. This noted Indian sachem Samorset, has left behind him a name in every way interesting and honorable. We first learn of him at Plymouth soon after the landing of the Pilgrims, when he was the first to welcome " The Pilgrim Fathers " to the inhospitable shores of Cape Cod. The natives feared and avoided them and until this time held no intercourse. The Pilgrims first unwisely incurred the enmity of the natives by their hostility in chasing them with fire arms upon their own shores, and threatening them with injury.

The Pilgrims at this time were in great peril, after their ship the Mayflower had departed, fearing destruction from their savage foes. He very boldly came among them and saluted them in English, and bade them " Much Welcome Englishmen. " Their account relates: " We questioned him of many things." His answer to them about the location of Pemaquid was significant, when he stated: "It lyeth hence a day's sail with a great wind, and five days by land," thus indicating there was an Indian trail leading along the New England shores as well as a waterway.

We have further evidence here of communication and traffic between the different tribes of New England, by the fine jasper arrow heads and chips, which we find in the Indian shell heap upon the banks of the Pemaquid River. I have never been able to learn of any other locality in New England where these choice pieces of flint can be obtained, except just west of the city of Lynn, Mass., where a vein of it crops out on the bank of the Saugus River, near the station at Saugus Centre.

Samorset was able to give them information by giving the names of the ships and their captains which had fished and traded at Pemaquid ports for many years. He could name the Chiefs of all the New England tribes and tell them the number of their warriors. Their description of him in the following words is interesting:

"The wind beginning to rise a little we cast a horseman's coat about him; for he was stark naked, only a leather about his waist, with a fringe about a span long or little more. He had a bow and two arrows, the one headed and the other unheaded. He was a tall, straight man; the hair of his head black, long behind, only short before; none on his face at all. He asked some beer, but we gave him strong water, and biscuit, and butter, and cheese, and pudding, and a piece of mallard; all of which he liked well, and had been acquainted with such amongst the English. * * * All the afternoon we spent in conversation with him."

Bradford says that "he came boldly amongst them and spoke to them in broken English, which they could well understand." He became profitable to them in acquainting them with many things concerning the state of the country in the east parts where he lived, which was afterwards profitable unto them.

Both of the writers just quoted proceed to show the various modes in which this interesting "savage" made himself "profitable" to them. He informed them of the hostility of the natives to the English, in consequence of Hunt's treachery some years before, and used his influence to produce a better state of feeling. He introduced to them his friend Squanto or Tisquantum, a native of the place who had been in England, and who afterwards became "a spetiall instrument sent of God for their good beyond their expectation."

Samorset continued in the vicinity some time, always seeking to promote good feeling between the English and the natives. This led to the formation of a treaty of peace between the new colony of Plymouth and Massasoit, sagamore of the neighboring Wampanoag Indians, which remained inviolate more than fifty years, or until the time of King Philip's war in 1675. Samorset probably returned soon after this to his native place, as we hear nothing further of him at Plymouth.

The next we hear of him he is at Capmanwagan (Capenewagen) on the coast of Maine, at the time of Levett's visit there, in the winter of 1623–4. Levett introduced him to us as a "sagamore that hath been found very faithful to the English, and hath saved the lives of many of our nation, some from starving, and others from killing." He received Levett with much cordiality, calling him cousin. He had become so much acquainted with the English as to be entirely free from the timidities usually shown by the natives at this early period, and proposed that perpetual friendship should be maintained between them, "until Tanto carried them to his wigwam, that is, until they died." He had his wife and son with him there, and several noble attendants. The simple narrative of Levett presents them before us in a very interesting light. His wife in particular conducted herself in true royal style.

"When we came to York the masters of the ships came to bid me welcome, and asked what savages those were. I told them, and I thanked them; they used them kindly, gave them meat, drink and tobacco. The woman, or reported queen, asked me if those men were my friends. I told her they were; then she drank to them, and told them they were welcome to her country, and so should all my friends be at any time. She drank also to her husband, and bid him welcome to her country too; for you must understand that her father was the Sagamore of this place, and left it to her at his death, having no more children."

Samorset lived many years after this in quiet and peaceable intercourse with his new neighbors; certain it is history records no quarrel between the parties! Samorset must at this time have been an old man, and probably soon passed away. Though an "untutored savage," he has left behind him a character highly creditable to him, as a man of elevated rank among his countrymen. He appears not only to have been destitute of the jealousies and petty vices of his race; but, at the same time, to have manifested on all occasions a love of justice and truth, a generous confidence in others, and an elevation of soul far superior to very many of the Europeans with whom he was brought in contact. The fact that as late as 1673 his name was still remembered among the natives as that of a "famous Sachem," shows that his manly character was not unappreciated by them.

In 1615, fierce wars broke out among the Indians, during which the great Bashaba of the Penobscot was slain, and probably his whole family was destroyed, for we hear no more of such a ruler in this region; then a dreadful pestilence broke out among the savages and continued for several years. At that time this great diminution of the native population favored the colonization of the country by Europeans.

CHAPTER X.

Pemaquid Patent.

AN important document called "The Patent," is deposited in the library of the American Antiquarian Society at Worcester, Mass.; it will take up too much room to copy in this sketch, but I will give the dates and name the parties interested in this document, because of its connection with the early history of this place, for a period of nearly two hundred years. It had the peculiar date at the heading, which reads as follows: "This Indenture made the Nine and twenteth day of February Anno D'm 1631, And in the Seaventh yeere of the Raigne of our Sovraigne Lord Charles by the grace of God King of England Scotland France and Ireland, Defender of the ffaith," etc.

This patent or deed conveyed twelve thousand acres of land at Pemaquid to Robert Aldsworth and Gyles Elbridge, merchants of Bristol, England. Capt. Walter Neale acted as agent of the grantors, and Mr. Abraham Shurte of Pemaquid, as agent for the grantees. Shem Drowne who constructed the noted grasshopper vane on Faneuil Hall at Boston, long acted as agent for the heirs-at-law who claimed this territory under the patent above spoken of.

Prof. Johnson, a native of Bristol and author of the history of Bristol and Bremen, says: "The deed of White and Davidson who afterwards came into possession of this patent, by which they conveyed it to others, are decided curiosities. They go wonderfully into details conveying to the grantee everything above and below, around and beneath, real and imaginary, pertaining to the place. The deed to White is a full warrantry, as we should call it at the present time; and the grantor engages ' to save and keep harmless and indemnifie, as well the said Paul White, his heirs, undertakes and assigns, and every of them, and all and singular the said premises, and from and concerning all other bargains, sales, joyntures, dowers, titles of dowers, arrearages of rents, and of the staple, exec[utive] judgments extents, forfeitures, charges, titles, troubles, incumbrances, and demands whatsoever,' etc."

Elbridge continued to reside at Pemaquid long after he had conveyed away all his right in the patent. In his conveyances he styled himself "merchant of Pemaquid." He was a man of small stature and insignificant appearance, but ever exerted a mild and beneficial influence in the settlement. But he was not permitted to live without molestation, for in 1659, he brought two actions against George Cleeve, one for defamation and the other for assault and battery, on the first of which he recovered fifty pounds damages. The result of the other action is not stated. He was still living in 1672, for we find his name as the signer of a petition from residents of the place, to be taken under the government and protection of Massachusetts. It is not known whether he had any family, nor has the time of his death been ascertained. Thomas Elbridge, who was a member of the first fire company formed in Boston, 1676, may have been the same man.

CHAPTER XI.

WRECK OF ANGEL GABRIEL AT PEMAQUID IN 1635.

"THE great storm of August 15, 1635, was probably one of the most severe and destructive ever known on the coast of New England. It ravaged the whole coast from Nova Scotia to Manhattan (New York) and probably further south. It began early in the morning with the wind at the northeast, and continued with great fury five or six hours, the tide rising in some places more than twenty feet 'right up and down.' According to some of the old writers, the tide not only rose to a very unusual height, but was attended by other peculiar circumstances. High tide seems to have occured about the proper time, according to calculation, and was followed by a partial ebb, but then immediately succeeded another and unaccountable tidal wave, in which the water rose even higher than at first. The growing crops everywhere were greatly injured, and the largest trees of the forest, which then covered a large part of the surface, were blown down in immense numbers.

"This storm was very severe at Pemaquid, but we are indebted chiefly to a disastrous shipwreck that occured here for what information we have of its ravages. June 22d, previously, two ships, the Angel Gabriel of two hundred and forty tons, and carrying sixteen guns, and the James of two hundred and twenty tons, sailed together from Milford Haven for New England; both bringing passengers and supplies for the colonies. They kept together for nearly two weeks, but the James, being the best sailer, at length lost sight of the other, and proceeded on her voyage. During those two weeks the latter had not spread all their sails, so that they 'might not overgo her.'

"Among the passengers of the James was the Rev. Richard Mather and family, the ancestors of Drs. Increase and Cotton Mather, and most or all of the name in New England. Both of the ships, besides their passengers, brought also cattle and other domestic animals, with the necessary supplies for the voyage. Mr. Mather kept a diary during the voyage, which was published by Dr. Young in his Chronicles of Massachusetts in 1846, after having been kept in manuscript two hundred and eleven years. Afterwards it was republished by the Dorchester Antiquarian and Historical Society.

"But though the James thus early in the voyage was obliged to part with her consort, because of her own fast sailing, she did not arrive much in advance of her. The great storm of Aug. 15th, found her at anchor at Isle of Shoals; but having, in the first part of it, lost all her anchors, she was obliged to put to sea again, and after a very perilous contest with the storm, and having all her sails 'rent in sunder and split in pieces, as if they had been rotten ragges,' arrived in Boston harbor the next day. Mr. Mather 'was exercised' as he expressed it, at least once every Sabbath, during the voyage, and sometimes at 'both ends of the day.'

"The night before the storm, while the James lay at the Isle of Shoals, the Angel Gabriel lay also at anchor at Pemaquid; but probably not in the inner harbor, for if she had been there, even if her anchors could not hold her, she could not have been dashed in pieces, as actually happened. One seaman and three or four of the passengers were lost, and most of the animals and goods. Of the latter, a part was recovered in a damaged state. Among the passengers by the Angel Gabriel was Mr. John Cogswell, a London merchant, who afterwards established himself in business at Ipswich. He was accompanied by three sons and several servants, and brought also many valuable household goods.

" The following deposition is of interest, as connected with the shipwreck. It is contained in the Massachusetts Archives, Vol. XXX; p. 535. A quarrel had arisen among the sons, or other descendants of Cogswell, which found its way into the courts; and this deposition was taken in reference to the trial; and probably was actually used. Another deposition of Wm. Furber, also servant of Cogswell, was taken the same day, and is of the same character. Mass. Archives, Vol. XXXIX, p. 504.

" The Deposition of William Furber, Senr., aged 60 years or there abouts.

" This Deponent testifyeth and saith, that in the year of our Lord 1635 I the said Deponent did come over in the ship (called the Angell Gabriel) along with Mr. John Cogswell Senr. from Old England, and we were cast ashore at Pemnay-quid; and I doe remember that there was saved several Casks both of Dry Goods and provisions which were marked with Mr. Cogswell Senr. Marks and that there saved a tent of Mr. Cogswell Senr. which he had set up at Pemnaquid, and Lived In it (with the goods that he saved in the wracke) and after-wards Mr. Cogswell Removed to Ipswich; And in november after that was cast away I the said Deponent Came to Ipswich and found Mr. Cogswell, Senr. Living there, and hired myself with him for one year; I the said Deponent doe well remem-ber that there were several feather beds and I together with Deacon Haines [ancestor of our Governor of Maine in 1913-14] as servants lay upon one of them, and there were several dozen of pewter platters, and that there were several brass pans besides other pieces of pewter and other household goods as Iron Worke and others necessary as for house Repairing and have in the house then. I the said Deponent doe further testify that there were two maires and two Cows brought over in another ship which were landed safe ashoare and were kept at misticke till Mr. Cogswell had y^{m}. I doe further testify that my maister, John Cogswell Senr. had three sons which came over along with us in the ship (called the Angell Gabriel) the

Eldest sonnes name were William, and he were about fourteen yeares of age, and the second sonne were called John and he was about twelve years of age then, and the third sonne name were Edward which was about six years of age at that time, and further saith not. William Furber Sen[r]. came and made oath to all the above written this first of Xber. (December) 1676. "Before me Richard Martyn, Comis[r].

" A fellow passenger with Mather on the Angel Gabriel, was Bailey, who came over to this country with the view of settling here, but left his wife in the old country, until he could first make himself a little acquainted with the new country, and provide a suitable place for his family. Though he escaped from the wreck unhurt, his mind was deeply affected by his narrow escape, and he wrote to his wife such a doleful account of the storm and shipwreck, that she never could be persuaded to undertake the voyage, even to join her husband. And he was too timid to risk himself again on the stormy Atlantic, they remained separate the rest of their lives."

Another account which has been kindly furnished me by Mrs. Martha A. Baker, gives more details of the affairs on board the James, the companion ship of the Angel Gabriel. From that we learn that the Angel Gabriel was built for Sir Walter Raleigh, sailed from Bristol, England, on June the fourth with servants, passengers and five of the six daughters of John Cogswell, in addition to the three sons mentioned in the above account; she also brought farming implements and considerable money and that they were twelve weeks and two days on the voyage.

We are interested in the Rev. Richard Mather, because he was a noted divine and his son Increase, once President of Harvard College, and to his grandson Cotton, we are indebted for a description of the first stone fort built at Pemaquid and for much of the early colonial history of New England. The Rev. Dr. Increase Mather states that " The Angel Gabriel was the first vessel which miscarried with passengers from Old

The Archangel, Capt. George Weymouth, the First Known Vessel Claiming Land at St. Georges Islands and Thomaston, by setting up English Crosses in 1605

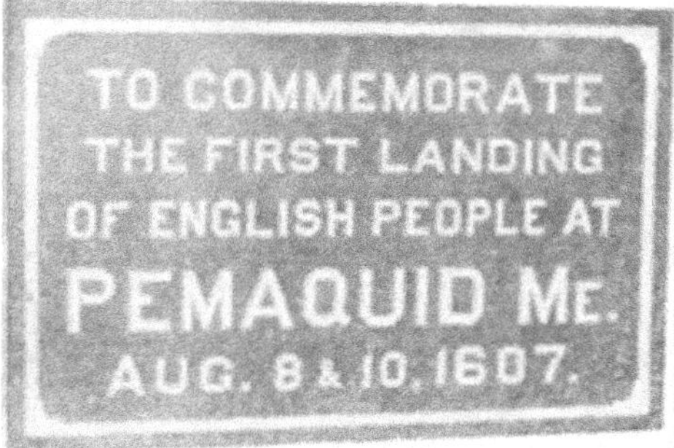

Tablet from Pemaquid, placed in Cape Cod Monument. This date is 13 Years Previous to Plymouth

Odd-shaped Brick used in the Construction of the old "Cashe"

England to New, so signally did the Lord in his providence watch over the plantations of New England." That seems the more remarkable when we consider that there were no lighthouses, buoys or beacons to guide the mariner clear of the sunken rocks or through safe channels to the harbors, as we have to-day. It seems to indicate that they had good ships and knew well how to manage them.

CHAPTER XII.

TROUBLE FOR PEMAQUID SETTLERS — TREATY OF ST. GERMAIN.

"TWO events occured in 1635 which caused uneasiness in all the New England colonies: the surrender of the charter of the Plymouth (Eng.) Council (consisting of forty noblemen and gentlemen of England); and the continued encroachments of the French from the eastward."

This territory was not divided, as to-day, into states; counties and towns. The rulers of England and France, when they gave their subjects titles to this territory, often overlapped each other. When their subjects came here a dispute arose about the boundaries. The English had established trading posts as far east as Castine and Machias, but they were broken up by the French who became so bold as to claim all the territory along the coast to Cape Cod. They claimed all the territory of Pemaquid as a part of Acadia. They fortified Castine and held it against an armed ship. "In this affair," says Prof. Johnson, "the Pemaquid settlers found themselves between two fires, for while the French on one hand, were threatening to displace them as intruders, on the other hand, Gov. Bradford of Plymouth complained that they 'filled ye Indians with guns and munishtion to the great danger of ye English,' and kept both the French and Indians informed of what was passing among the colonists. Their position was exceedingly critical, but their affairs seem to have been managed with great skill and moderation; so that if they did not altogether please the three parties, viz., the English colonies west of them, the French at the east, or the native Indians, in their midst, they at least gave mortal offense to none. As a natural result, they for many years enjoyed a good degree of prosperity, and the population of the place rapidly increased. Gov. Winthrop, in a very incidental manner, affords us some evidence of the prosperity of the place, in the month of May, 1640. 'Joseph Grafton set sail from Salem, the second day in the morning, in a ketch of about forty tons, (three men and a boy in her) and arrived at Pemaquid (the wind easterly) upon the third day (Tuesday) in the morning, and then took in some twenty cows, oxen, etc., with hay and oats for them, and came to an anchor in the bay the 6th day about three afternoon.'

"This was making good despatch, but the voyage could very easily be accomplished in the time mentioned, if the vessel was only a moderately good sailer, and the wind favorable both going and returning.

"In 1636, cows sold in Massachusetts as high as twenty-five and even thirty pounds a head, and oxen at forty pounds per pair, but after this the price was lower."

Two vigorous but unprincipled Frenchmen, one named Charles Etienne La Tour, a professed Protestant, and M. D'Aulney de Charnisse a catholic, for twelve years caused trouble at Pemaquid. The former took Machias and the latter captured Castine by strategy. These two men had been granted titles to much land at Acadia. On the death of Gen. Razilly, their superior commander, a rivalry sprung up between them which soon became a bitter quarrel, that threatened all the English settlements on the coast.

D'Aulney confided in the French government for assistance, and his rival in the Protestant colonies along the coast. The king of France, Louis XIV, authorized D'Aulney to arrest La Tour and send him back a prisoner to France. This order intensified the strife and they fought like two independent chieftains. In 1641 La Tour by his agent applied to Massachusetts for aid against his rival, who carried a letter of introduction from Abraham Shurte of Pemaquid. He finally got permission to hire ships and enlist men at his own expense, and secured four ships and one hundred forty-two men as sailors and soldiers, but the English colony being a government not wishing to incur the displeasure of D'Aulney, would not openly assist him though they sympathized with him. La Tour was established at St. John and D'Aulney at Castine, and kept up their struggle.

In the spring of 1645 D'Aulney learned that La Tour was absent from his garrison; he proceeded then to attack it. On the way he met a New England vessel and made a prize of her in utter disregard of a treaty he had just made with the English colonists, turned the crew ashore on a distant island without food or suitable clothing. On arriving at St. John he bombarded the fort, but Madam La Tour who had commanded during her husband's absence, made such spirited resistance that he was obliged to retire, his ship being badly damaged, with twenty of his men killed and thirteen wounded. On his return, a wiser, if not a better man, he took aboard the men he had put ashore on the island, who had remained there ten days in great suffering, and gave them an old shallop to return in, but without restoring any of their property.

Finally this miserable quarrel was brought to a close. In April, 1647, D'Aulney again suddenly made his appearance at St. John and attacked the fort with so much energy that he soon gained possession of it, making Madame La Tour and the whole garrison prisoners, and appropriating to himself all of La Tour's effects of every kind, which was not less than ten thousand pounds.

Madame La Tour, in the absence of her husband, had command of the fort, and, as on a former, similar occasion, defended it with great vigor, killing and wounding many of D'Aulney's men, but the latter, having gained some advantage, offered favorable terms. She was induced to capitulate, surrendering everything into the hands of her adversary. As soon as possession of the fort had been gained, D'Aulney, utterly disregarding the promises he had made, in accordance with his base nature, put the whole garrison to death, except one man, and compelled Madame La Tour herself, with a rope around her neck, to be present at the execution. This lady, exhausted by the heroic exertions she had made in defending the fort, and stung to madness by the wrongs and indignities she was made to suffer, died three weeks after the surrender of the fort.

Her husband, now reduced to poverty, was left a wanderer and an exile. At this time La Tour owed considerable sums to individuals in Massachusetts, to whom much of his property in Nova Scotia was mortgaged, one man alone, by name of Gibbons, having a claim of more than £2,500. The prospects of ever collecting their dues were now small. La Tour in despair now made application for aid to his former friend, Sir David Kirk of Newfoundland, but without effect. He then turned again to Massachusetts, where he found some men of wealth who, still having confidence in his integrity, furnished him with a vessel and goods to the value of £400, for a trading excursion among the Indians at the east.

Arriving at Cape Sable, he developed his true character as a low scoundrel and hypocrite, by entering into a conspiracy with a part of his crew, who were Frenchmen, to put ashore the others who were English, taking possession of the vessel and cargo as their own. The men, thus put ashore in the depth of winter, in a destitute condition, were, after much suffering, relieved by a party of Mickmack Indians, who kindly aided them in returning to their homes. La Tour and his confederates, now regular pirates, it is believed, sailed farther east to Hudson's Bay; but nothing is known of their doings. D'Aulney died in 1651, which opened a way for La Tour's return to the scene of his former exploits.

The ferocious contest between these two unscrupulous rivals, raged with more or less violence for twelve years, and produced effects not a little detrimental to the settlement at Pemaquid, and all others on the coast. Sometimes enormous wrongs were committed on innocent people, living in the neighborhood, by their exploits; angry menaces occasionally thrown out, could not but excite the apprehensions of the persons living so near as Pemaquid.

But stranger things connected with this affair remain yet to be mentioned. La Tour, after his return, made love to the widow of his late hated rival, D'Aulney; and they were actually married, and lived together many years, several children being born to them. All his former possessions in Nova Scotia were now resumed by him, and a singular prosperity marked the latter years of his life: but it is added, in the history of the time, that in all his prosperity he did not remember his friends in Massachusetts, who aided him in the days of his adversity and trial, so much as to pay them the money he owed them. So singular a termination to such a bitter and protracted contest exceeds the limits of ordinary romance; and one scarcely knows whether it should be contemplated as belonging "to the sublime or ridiculous, to the romantic or the disgusting."

CHAPTER XIII.

PEMAQUID UNDER THE DUKE OF YORK — THE FIRST INDIAN WAR AT PEMAQUID CALLED KING PHILIP'S WAR.

1664 – 1686.

SEVERAL years ago, while hunting in an old bookstore at Boston, I fortunately secured a copy of a volume of records pertaining to Pemaquid, compiled by Franklin B. Hough. "In 1664, the Duke of York received from his brother, King Charles, a grant of the territory of New York, including Martha's Vineyard and Nantucket, and also the territory in Maine extending from the St. Croix on the East to the Kennebec on the West. The latter, which included Pemaquid, was named Cornwall. The governors appointed to rule over the territory being located at New York, seem not to have given much attention to this part of their possessions until after the terrible war of King Philip began in 1676.

The first fierce Indian war which burst with fury upon Pemaquid and the neighboring settlements in 1676, was a part of the same great struggle which the year before raged in Massachusetts and is known in history as King Philip's war. A full half century had elapsed since the settlement at Pemaquid was begun. Then began that fearful struggle for the existence of each nation, the echoes of which have been handed down to us to this day by tradition."

When wild the war-whoop clave the quivering air,
  With crash of cannon and the trumpet's clang,
When wails of woman and the voice of prayer
  With moans of death through fair Mavooshen rang.

The frantic mother wept and prayed in vain,
  While savage hands the smiling infant slew,
And burning ruin smoked along the plain,
  So wild, so sharp the fiendish warfare grew;
And o'er the land pale Fear with Famine crept,
  Dark Desolation's slow and silent train.

Then sad and lingering was the sure decay,
  That dragged the dying city to its doom,
Till this fair valley where we walk to-day,
  From hill to river, blossoms o'er a tomb;
The happy homes so bright, so full of song,
  Lie mouldering here beneath the crumbling clay;
The happy hearts, with faith and courage strong,
  Sleep on beside them, cold and still as they.

M. W. Hackelton.

"They first begun here by gratifying their revenge, but ended in an indiscriminate slaughter of friends as well as foes. The Indian depredation began September 20, 1675, against the settlers for undertaking to deprive them of their guns and ammunition to prevent them from using them against the whites; they resented this because they had become so accustomed to the use of the musket as to be largely dependent upon it for obtaining their daily food.

Some have doubted whether the outbreak of the eastern Indians had any connection with King Philip's war but the connection of the two is too plain to need argument. In the course of the war, several Narragansett Indians were actually captured in arms with their brethren at the east."

"On June 13, 1677, Gov. Andros of N. York, sent four good sloops here loaded with lumber and other material for a strong Redoubt. Lieu. Anthony Brockholls, Ensign Cesar Knapton, and Mr. M. Nickolls had command of the expedition. On their arival they prosceeded to erect the fortification and named it Fort Charles."

The fortifications erected at this time consisted of "a wooden Redout wth two guns aloft and an outworke with two Basions in each of wch two greatt guns, and one att ye Gate; fifty souldiers wth sufficient ammunicon, stores of warre, and spare arms, victualled for about eight months, and his Roy[ll] Highness sloope wth four gunns to attend ye Coast and fishery."

This wooden fort or redoubt occupied very nearly the same site as those erected subsequently, but was situated a little east of the rock, as will hereafter appear. Capt. Anthony Brockholls and Ensign Cæsar Knapton were put in command of the fort and settlements, with a company of fifty soldiers. They called the place Jamestown in honor of the King, James II. As soon as the duke's government was established, orders were at once given for the regulation of trade and nearly all of the other affairs of the settlement. All questions of disagreement between the inhabitants and fishermen to be referred to a justice of the peace, an appeal being allowed in important cases to the governor at New York.

At a Councell Sept. 27, 1677, Held at New York, The Orders and Directions were made for the Commander of Pemaquid as follows:

The trading place to be at Pemaquid and no where else.

All entryes to bee made at New Yorke and no Coasters or Interlopers allowed, but if any found to be made prise.

Liberty of stages (places for drying and taking care of fish) upon the Islands but not upon the Maine, except at Pemaquid near the fort.

The Indyans not to goe to ye fishing Islands.

No rum to bee dranke on that side the ffort stands.

No man to trust any Indyans.

Traders from New York were allowed to establish houses in the place, but only near the fort and on a street of good breadth leading directly from the Fort to the narrowest part of the neck or point of land the Fort stands upon, going to the great neck towards New Harbor.

All trade to be in the said Street, in or afore the houses, between sun and sun, for which the drum to beate, or bell ring every morning and evening, and neither Indyan nor Christian suffered to drink any strong drinks nor lye ashore in the night, &c.

No Indyans nor Christians to be Admitted att any time within the Fort except some few upon occasion of businesse below, but none to goe up into the Redout, &c.

Fishermen giving notice to the Fort to have all Liberty of taking their fish on the fishing Islands, or neare and under protection of the Fort.

If Occasion one or more Constables to be appointed for the fishing Islands, and Indyans to have equal Justice and Dispatch.

Fishermen to come to Pemaquid yearly to renew their Engagen and not to splitt or fling out their Gurry on the fishing grounds, or to trade with the Indyans to the prejudice of the fishery and hazard of these part.

Any Trader or other trusting an Indyan or Indyans except for dry provissings, or adulterating Rumme or strong drinke by mixing water or otherwise, to forfet the same to the party trusted or buying, and be lyable to further censure as the Case may require and the forfeiture of the remaining part of such strong Liquor to be to Commander, satisfying or paying the informer.

Land to bee given out indifferently to those that shall come and settle, but no trade to bee at any place than Pemaquid, and none at all with the Indyans as formerly ordered.

It shall not be Lawful for any Vessels crew that belongeth not to the Government to make a voyage in the Government, except he hath an house or stage within the Government on penalty of forfeiture of paying for making his voyage.

It shall not be lawful for fishermen to keep any more dogges than one to a family on such penalty and forfeiture as shall be thought fitt by you [Capt. of the Fort.]

No coasting vessels shall trade on the Cost as Bum boats tradeing from Harbor to Harbor, but as shall supply the Generall account for one boat or more, neither shall it be lawful for him to trade in any other Harbor, but where the boat or boats are, neither shall it be lawful for him to trade with any other crew for liquors or wine, Rumm, Beer, Sider, &c., on such penalty as you [Capt. of Fort] think fitting.

All vessels out of any Government if they come to trade or fish shall first enter at Pemaquid, or the places appointed, and they shall not go in any other Harbor, except by stress of weather. No stragling farmes shall be erected, nor no houses built any where under the number of twenty.

[A REDUCED FACSIMILE OF A PROCLAMATION ISSUED BY ANDROS WHILE IN MAINE IN 1688.]

BY HIS EXCELLENCY
A
PROCLAMATION.

WHEREAS His MAJESTY hath been graciously pleased, by His Royal Letter, bearing Date the sixteenth day of October last past, to signifie That He hath received undoubted Advice that a great and sudden Invasion from *Holland*, with an armed Force of Forreigners and Strangers, will speedily be made in an hostile manner upon His Majesty's Kingdom of *ENGLAND*; and that altho' some *false* pretences relating to *Liberty*, *Property*, and *Religion*, (contrived or worded with Art and Subtilty) may be given out, (as shall be thought useful upon such an Attempt;) It is manifest however, (considering the great preparations that are making) That no less matter by this *Invasion* is proposed and purposed, than an absolute Conquest of His Majesty's Kingdoms, and the utter Subduing and Subjecting His Majesty and all His People to a Forreign Power, which is promoted ((as His Majesty understands) altho' it may seem almost incredible) by some of His Majesty's *Subjects*, being persons of wicked and restless Spirits, implacable Malice, and desperate Designs, who having no senec of former intestine Distractions, (the Memory and Misery whereof should endear and put a Value upon that Peace and Happiness which hath long been enjoyed) nor being moved by his Majesty's reiterated Acts of Grace and Mercy, (wherein His Majesty hath studied and delighted to abound towards all His Subjects, and even towards *those* who were once His Majesty's avowed and open *Enemies*) do again endeavour to embroil His Majesty's Kingdom in Blood and Ruin, to gratifie their own Ambition and Malice, proposing to themselves a Prey and Booty in such a publick Confusion:

And that although His Majesty had notice that a forreign Force was preparing against Him, yet his Majesty hath alwaies declined any foreign Succour, but rather hath chosen (next under GOD) to rely upon the true and ancient Courage, Faith and Allegiance of His own People, with whom His Majesty hath often ventured His Life for the Honour of His Nation, and in whose Defence against all Enemies His Majesty is firmly resolved to live and dye; and therefore does solemnly *Conjure* His Subjects to lay aside all manner of Animosities, Jealousies, & Prejudices, and heartily & chearfully to *Unite together* in the Defence of His *MAJESTY* and their native Countrey, which thing alone, will (under GOD) defeat and frustrate the principal Hope and Design of His Majesty's Enemies, who expect to find His People divided; and by publishing (perhaps) some plausible Reasons of their Coming, as the specious (tho' *false*) Pretences of Maintaining the Protestant Religion, or Asserting the Liberties and Properties of His Majesty's People, do hope thereby to conquer that great and renowned Kingdom.

That albeit the Design hath been carried on with all imaginable Secresie & Endeavours to surprise and deceive His *MAJESTY*, He hath not been wanting on His part to make such provision as did become Him, and, by GOD's great Blessing, His Majesty makes no doubt of being found in so good a Posture that His Enemies may have cause to repent such their rash and *unjust* Attempt. ALL WHICH, it is His Majesty's pleasure, should be made known in the most publick manner to His loving Subjects within this His Territory and Dominion of *NEW-ENGLAND*, that they may be the better prepared to resist any attempts that may be made by His Majesties Enemies in these parts, and secured in their trade and Commerce with His Majesty's Kingdom of *England*.

I Do therefore, in pursuance of His *MAJESTY'S* Commands, by these Presents *make known* and *Publish* the same accordingly; And hereby Charge and Command all Officers Civil & Military, and all other His Majesty's loving Subjects within this His Territory and Dominion aforesaid, to be *Vigilant* and *Careful* in their respective places and stations, and that, upon the Approach of any Fleet or Foreign Force, they be in Readiness, and use their utmost Endeavour to hinder any Landing or Invasion that may be intended to be made within the same.

Given at *Fort-Charles* at *Pemaquid*, the Tenth Day of *January*, in the Fourth year of the Reign of our Sovereign Lord *James* the Second, of *England*, *Scotland*, *France* and *Ireland* KING, Defender of the Faith &c. Annoq; DOMINI 1688.

By His EXCELLENCY's *Command*.

JOHN WEST. &. Secr'. E ANDROS

GOD *SAVE THE* KING.

Printed at *Boston* in *New-England* by R. P.

The above extracts from orders issued at different times show the general character of many more sent here for the military government of this place. The ruler of England, James II., and the Duke of York, were working through their agent, Sir Edmond Andros, to bring the colonists more fully under their control and make them pay more tribute to the crown. They also meant to punish the other New England colonies, by excluding them from trade with the Indians, or taking fish on the coast except by payment of tribute at the Pemaquid custom house.

In December, 1680, Thomas Sharpe was appointed Captain of the Fort, and Francis Skinner August 30, 1681. Other officers, civil and military, were appointed from time to time by the governor. Among the names we find Henry Jocelyn, was chosen " to bee Justice of the Peace in Corum " [Quorum]. Other justices in Cornwall were John Dollin, Lawrenc Dennis, John Jourdain, Richard Redding, John Allen, Thomas Giles or [Gyles], Alexander Waldorp, Thomas Sharp, Richard Pattishall, Nicholas Manning, Giles Goddard, Ceasor Knapton, John West and Elihu Gunnison. Sheriffs, constables, and other officers were appointed but their names are not preserved with those above.

Many letters and documents, contained in that volume of ancient records are interesting. One letter to the commander of the fort speaks of sending thirty pounds to buy a sailing shallop, and cautions him to " Take care to keepe the platforme in the fort in good repaire wch I judge you doe by wattering or throwing stuffe or earth thereupon." The details for care of guns, store, traffic with the natives, etc., are wonderful accounts of what was to be forwarded by Gov. Andros. One letter from Capt. Brockholls dated New York, May 10th, 1683, to Mr. Francis Skinner reads:

" I am sorry the loossness and carelessness of your command gives oppertunity for strangers to take notice of your extraviganyes and Debaucheryes and that complaints must come to me thereoff being what your Office and Place ought to prevent and punish. Expect a better observance and comporte for the future and that Swearing, Drinking and profaneness to much practiced and Suffered with you will be wholly Suppressed and that you have Regard to all former Orders and Regulations."

Your Affectionate friend,

A. B.

Col. Thomas Dongan was appointed to succeed Andros in 1682, and arrived in this country in August, 1683. A long petition was soon sent to him by the inhabitants of a part of Cornwall containing eight articles and reciting their grievances under Andros and praying for relief. It was signed by eighteen persons.

Also a petition directly relating to this locality was sent in this form:—

"To the Right honerable Governor and Council of Assembly of New Yorke. The humble Petition of New Harbor humbly sheweth: That, whereas yor petitioners have been at great charge in building their habitations, and as yet have noe assurance of either house lots or the bounds of our place, which is a hindrance to our conveniencyes of planting or making an improvement, etc. We humbly [pray] that there may be surveyors appointed for that purpose to lay out lands; likewise the * * * of these customs may be taken off, because it never used to be paid by any ffisherman in this world as we know of, and it hinders the coasters comming to us to bring our supplies, and when they do come, the very name of these customs makes them sell their goods almost as dear again as formerly they used, so that we finde it to be to all the countrye a grevious burden and to all the people called fishermen an utter ruin.

AND THAT PEMAQUID MAY STILL REMAIN THE METROPOLITAN OF THESE PARTS, BECAUSE IT EVER HAVE BEEN SO BEFORE BOSTON WAS SETTLED. Wherfore your honers poor petitioners humbly desire that the honorable Governor and Councell would please to take the premises into your pious consideration, to order and confirm the lots, bounds, limits of this place to be laid out, and that we may enjoy the labors of our hands and have it for our children after us, and also that the customs may be taken of, and raised some other way, and that *Pemaquid may be the metropolitan (metropolis) place*, and your honers petitioners as in duty bound shall ever pray.

Per order of the inhabitants,

WM. STUART, *Town Clerk at Pemaquid.*

By the following orders sent here by Governor Dongan to Capt. Nicholas Manning, the "Sub-Collector, Surveyor, &c., for these parts," the earliest stringent liquor laws of Maine must have been enforced at Old Pemaquid. Among fourteen articles for the government of the fisheries collections of "quit rents," customs, etc.; the seventh and eighth articles read as follows:

"7thly. You are to goe into ye house & Cellar of any p^{r}son or p^{r}sons whatsoever where ye suspect there is any wine or other liquors & Syder that shall be by them sold & retailed. You are alsoe to goe into their Cellars & houses as afores^{d} as yo^{u} shall see Cause to p^{r}vent all fraud & Imbezellment of his Maties Revenue.

8thly. You are not to suffer any Vessell whatsoever to goe into or up Kenebeque River or any parte thereof until they have first made their entry with yo^{u} at Jamestown & payed his Maties Dews & if any shall presume to doe ye Contrary y^{o} are to Cause both vessell & Goods to be Seized & proceeded ags^{t} by Law as directed for defrauding his Matie of his Customes. And that all Vessells tradeing into any porte River or place doe Enter & Cleere with yo^{u} before there departure und^{r} the like pains & forfeitures.

10thly. You are not to suffer any p^{r}son or p^{r}sons to sell any sort of Liquors by retaile in any part or place within ye s^{d} County but such as shall obtaine Lycence from yo^{r}selfe & shall pay such sume of mony for ye Same as yo^{u} shall think fitt to agree for & not lesse than 12^{s} for Each Lycence g^{r}ted and of ye monys on that behalfe received yo^{u} are to Render a p^{r}ticular ac^{t} to ye Govr as opportunity p^{r}sents."

When at the death of King Charles II. the Duke of York became King James II., changes of government occurred by which was established "the territory and dominion of New England." Then for convenience Pemaquid was detached from New York and annexed to Massachusetts.

The following "Royal Order" directs this transfer of jurisdiction.

JAMES R.

Trusty & well beloved wee Greet you well. Whereas wee have thought fitt to direct that our ffort & Country of Pemaquid in regard of its distance from New York bee for the future annexed to & Continued under the Governmt of our territory & dominion of New England our will & pleasure is that you forthwith Deliver or cause to be delivered our said ffort & Country of Pemaquid with the Greate Gunns, ammunicon & stores of warr together with all other utensils & appurtennces belonging to the said ffort into the hands of our trusty and welbeloved Sir Edmund Andross Knight our Captaine Generall & Governour in chief of our territory & dominion of New England or to the Governor or Commander in Chiefe there for the time being or to such person or persons as they shall Impower to receive the same and for soe doing this shall be your warrant.

Given at our Court at windsor this 19th day of Sept., 1686 & in the second yeare of our Reigne.

By his Ma[ties] Command,

SUNDERLAND, CL. [Clerk]

The following note was printed below this order :

The Great Guns from the fort at Pemaquid, after being carried to Boston, were by order of the King in the spring of 1691, transferred to New York. (N. Y. Coll. MSS. xxxvii.)

[Under the heading of "Passes" we find the following list of vessels that were granted dispatch to sail for Pemaquid.]

[Pass Book IV.]

Dispatch granted to the Barke Elizabeth Alizander Woodrop Master bound for Pemaquid November ye 29th 83.

Dispatch granted to the sloope Happy Returne, James Barry Commander for Pemaquid & New found Land Aprill 26th 1684.

Despatch granted to the Sloope Blossom Stephen Heacock Comander for Pemaquid May the 22d 1685.

Despatch granted to the Sloope Prinrose John Eurest Master for Stratford and off Pemaquid New York July the 4th 1685.

Despatch granted to the sloope Lewis Frances Bassett Comander for Pemaquid & New found Land [Sept. 4 (?) 1685.]

Despatch granted to the Sloope Adventurer Thomas Brookes Commander for Boston & Pemaquid, June 19th 1686.

Lucas Andries Masr of the sloop Elias enters the sd sloop for Pemaquid with Contents of Loading. [June 20, 1681.]

Lawrence Sluce Enters the sloop Hopewell himself Master ffor Pemaquid with Contents of Loading. [Sept. 10, 1681.]

Stephen Hiskott mar of the Sloop Blossome Enters the sd Sloope for Pemaquid with Contents of Loading. [Oct. 21, 1681.]

CHAPTER XIV.

Relics of Pemaquid.

SOME years ago I published a small circular containing a list of the most important places and objects of interest which I had been able to trace out and obtain information about, over the ruins of this little historic peninsula. Having had further time to gather information from outside sources and personal examination here, I will try to give the reader the benefit of my researches.

I hope that no one who reads this account or comes here for investigation will be impressed with the idea that here are to be found grand old ruins of some great city like those of eastern lands where nations have risen, flourished and decayed; leaving behind them,

> Storied columns in massive grandeur piled,
> Above and underneath the soil, in ruin wild.

Here we have only the footprints of a nation's beginning. All along our seacoast those footprints can be found from this place to Jamestown, Virginia, spots where colonists found a stepping stone to rest upon after crossing the western ocean, and from which they have taken long and rapid strides until they have reached the broad Pacific Ocean.

Not all historic events of great importance have any relics left to mark where they occured. Just where Columbus landed is not known to-day, yet a World's Fair held at Chicago in 1892, celebrated the event.

Massachusetts, after nobly marking all her well known places of historic interest, starts out to mark with cairns historic spots where once stood some of her noted citizens to

The Old Fort Rock of Pemaquid, as it Appeared in 1893, After the Foundation Walls About It Had Been Buried and Forgotten

watch an important event. No wonder her children know the history of their State, and it must be admitted that ours of old Maine learn more of theirs than of their own from history.

What have we of old Maine done to preserve our ancient history, and mark our spots of historic interest? Why, Col. Dickey once at the State House at Augusta, when I inquired if he knew of any one there interested in ancient history, answered, "No! I never saw any one here that was interested in anything ancient;" said he, "I had hard work to get an appropriation to save our old block house at Fort Kent." He was a member of the legislature.

When I first came here to reside at the Jamestown Hotel I met Capt. George Johnson, who then boarded there with his daughter, Mrs. Addie Partridge, wife of the proprietor. Capt. Johnson for many years followed the sea, and during the latter part of his life took much interest in all the schools of our town and in all good work of Christianity and education. He loaned me two excellent books containing much information about this locality: the "History of Bristol and Bremen" and a poem by Mrs. Maria W. Hackelton, entitled "Jamestown of Pemaquid." Those two books gave me an inspiration to investigate the hidden mysteries of Old Pemaquid, which has never died out and I trust never will until with the kind assistance of others, we shall be able to show to our own citizens and to the world that Old Pemaquid was once of some account. I once heard a visitor say that "Pemaquid was of no account because it was not a *permanent settlement*." I trust that I may be able to prove that his remark was not correct.

CHAPTER XV.

Old Fort Rock, Castle and House.

NO better opportunity than that presented from the top of this Castle to view the middle point of land which comprises one of the three which form the southern part of the town of Bristol, and is bounded on the west by the John's river, and on the east by the celebrated winding river of Pemaquid. About one mile distant, on the opposite high bank, where the river makes a turn at right angles towards the west, an artificial mound is to be seen, at the top of the high hill, quite plainly from here. Although the relics hunters and different owners of the land have for many years been attempting to solve the mystery surrounding this locality, they have only made it more obscure by their promiscuous efforts. By communication with many people now passed away, by and examination of many relics seen and obtained, I am well convinced that once a small colony of intelligent white people occupied this spot of earth for a considerable time. Who they were, where they came from, how they disappeared, or when, can only be conjectured today by what they have left upon the shore. There is yet to be seen the remains of a small fortification formed by enclosing space with a stone wall and filling around it to the top with soil as a means of defence. The Eastern end was circular in form and arched to the top so it was covered with a large flat stone, which has been hauled away to use in the construction of the foundation of a house at Pemaquid Falls, also many of the Flag stones (flat stones used in covering the bottoms of the numerous cellars most likely, before the custom of cementing was practiced). The indica-

Fort Rock of Pemaquid, showing 8 ft. of the Castle, discovered 1893, forming the West corner of Fort Wm. Henry, and found strong enough to build upon when the Castle was restored in 1907-8. Old Fort House at left, built 1729

Six feet of the Front Wall of the Fort, as discovered about 1894, originally 6 feet thick and 22 feet high

tions of another structure, most likely a stockade, are plainly visible extending to the west from that already described. There are about seventy feet of paved street in close proximity to the former fort, extending down toward the shore, with three nicely walled cellars on one side of it. There was until recently a long stone by the wall of one cellar, which was evidently used for a step to the door. This paving though much narrower than that found on this side of the river, was apparently well laid with a good gutter or water course on the side of it. A few years since, Miss Cinthy Horsford, whose father built the tower at Norumbega Park in Massachusetts, employed Rev. Henry O. Thayer to make investigations at this place which he did by employing a man to excavate for two days in one of the old cellars which are nearly filled with dirt now. He was rewarded by finding the stone wall still in good shape, laid in a mortar not familiar to our masons today, and none of them can surpass its workmanship. In the corner of the one cellar excavated was found a broken Crock of earthen ware, odd brick, an old style hammer, and thirteen articles of use by civilized people, including glass, fragments of brick, hand made nails, a fine whet stone, fragments of crockery, part of a large door latch, and other iron implements which we do not know the name of, or what use they could have been put to in bygone days. The farm on which these remains are located was called the Lewis farm when I first knew of it, owned by Mr. Nathan Lewis, who had a large family of boys and girls. One of these boys used to dig about this old fort in company with Capt. L. D. McLain, when a young man, just to satisfy their curiosity. He informed me that while digging on the inside walls of the fort, which then were so high that they just came even with his chin, they used to find large fragments of crockery, and he secured cannon balls larger than those found on this side of the river. His most valuable prize was an old Machete like those used by the Spanish in our late war with them in Cuba. It was well wrapped in some preserving material, and proved to be made of good material, as Mr. McClain informed me that he had fastened it into a vice, and bent the end over until it was at a right angle with the side of the blade, without breaking, and then cut nails off with it without turning the edge. This instrument was 3 1-2 feet long, and had the letter H. stamped on one side of the blade. Unfortunately, this article and others was sold to Mr. Weatherby of Warren to add to his collection of curiosities, like hundreds of others found at various times at this place, which are now so scattered that it would be impossible to ever gather them up again. I have been shown a finely carved stone of bright red color, which was evidently a piece of jewelry, large keys, many small pipes, tileing and a large amount of other material, and a mineral formation of broken shells cemented together by some natural process, which can be found in no place on our shores nearer than Florida. Other remains of interest were those of a blacksmith shop, a tannery from which Mr. George N. Lewis secured a piece of tanned hide. A remarkably large cellar from which Capt. Will Davis, who purchased the farm of Mr. Lewis, showed me a drain leading from those tan pits to the shore, which we measured and found to be 350 feet long and 4 feet square. I do not think any building in the town today would require as many stones for a foundation. A deep well is said to have existed near the fortification. Unfortunately the Captain had the timber of those tan pits all excavated and hauled to the bank of the river, where the tides, or ice, had taken them away before I knew of their loss as interesting relics.

Across this river, opposite these remains, to the east, is a small cove, with steep bank on the north side of a little brook which empties there. About this outlet are remains of several old cellars, from which have been secured many relics of interest, consisting of parts of old guns, bullets, flints, small shot, several of them unattached, showing that they were run in a mould as bullets were at that time, a cleaver, large keys, and many other things mingled with broken arrow heads and

Old Fort Rock with Temporary Museum, as it Appeared Before the State Furnished the Funds to Rebuild the Castle

Indian implements which would seem to indicate former contention between the occupants of this territory. From the cellar extending down the bank towards the water's edge was a fine stone paving, which indicates that the pavings here as elsewhere in this vicinity led to what was the former highways of the early settlers, when the land was thickly covered with great forests. The rivers, bays, and creeks must have afforded them their easiest way of traveling in their boats. Many old cellars on both banks of this river, and others of unknown age and occupancy, still exist to prove the early settlement of this place. My theory of belief about this small fort is that it was a settlement of the Spanish, judging from the relics found there. The Machete found there, the underground passage, supposed to lead to the shore, the Coquina, and other things, seem to be indications of that people. In the year 1565 they had erected a strong fort at great expense at St. Augustine, Florida, which naturally must have required a great quantity of supplies from across the ocean. When those supplies were discharged the owners of those vessels would naturally seek something for a return cargo beside ballast. That nation, the French, and Portugese, we are informed, were engaged in fishing along these shores long before any attempt was made to settle the country; they came here in their ships and remained all through the summer. Those vessels which took goods to St. Augustine must have had ballast to make them safe to reach this shore, and this Coquina seems to have been the most convenient material to be obtained. When that was discharged here they could load with a cargo of fish or furs that would be a source of profit to them. In those times the habits of most nations, especially the Spanish, when they came to this country, was to intimidate the natives by acts of wanton cruelty, as history informs us of a native of the West Indies who was lashed to a tree so that an officer could cut the poor victim to pieces to test the temper of his sword. And another had nine natives bound in front of each other to test his power with a spear while riding on horseback; he penetrated seven of them. If the people who settled there attempted that custom they doubtless found their match among the native Warwenocks of this region, for the name indicated "Fear nothing." At any rate no tale of history has yet come down to us to even tell the name of their village or their fate.

Nearer to us on the high, spruce covered top at the north side of our harbor, which is cleared from the summit to the shore, are the fine buildings and estate formerly owned by Capt. Ambrose Child who, with another sea captain residing near Damariscotta, competed with each other to see who would get the best looking estate. We think that Capt. Child was the winner, but, unfortunately, he did not long survive to enjoy it. Sailing from New York in his ship, loaded with wheat for England, about 1862 or 63, with one of his own sons and several other young men from this town, his career was ended, and all must have been swallowed up by the sea, like many who have gone before and left no mark to tell us where or how they perished. Such a fate seems sad. This place afterwards came into the possession of Mr. Charles P. Thibbetts, who named it, very appropriately, the Bay View House, and accommodated many people there during the summer. In 1912 he passed away, and his son, William, ran it. During the last season it was let to a family by the name of Ireland, friends of Annie Russell. A large summer hotel kept by Mr. William Thibbetts, called the Edgemere, was located on this high shore a little further to the west, which was well patronized for several years until burned, to our disappointment.

The view to be obtained from the location of these houses we do not think can be surpassed on our New England shores. It was said by Mr. John Kelley of Philadelphia, when stopping at the Edgemere a few years ago, although he had visited all the noted resorts across the ocean and in this country, he

Castle at the West Corner of Fort William Henry, Originally Built Around the Fort Rock to Prevent the Indians from Using it Against the Settlement, as Formerly in Capturing Fort Charles. All the Land to be Seen from the Top of this Castle is a Part of Pemaquid

had seen no view to surpass that from the cupalo of the Edgemere, except that of the Thousand Islands of the St. Lawrence River. Other people have made similar expressions when witnessing the beautiful scenery, a combination of evergreen and deciduous trees, the waters of the inner and outer harbors, the bay and ocean dotted over with moving vessels, large and small, and islands extending as far as the eye can behold.

Directly opposite the Castle and mouth of the harbor are seen many cottages, most of which belong to people with permanent homes up the Kennebec river, near Augusta and Waterville, some of them from Massachusetts and some from New York; the one nearest to the shore was formerly occupied by Mr. John Stinson, then by Capt. Charles Sproul, then by Mr. Frank C. Penny, who with his wife moved to California, and they both died there within a few years. Mr. Penny sold the place to Mr. John Carty of New York City, a brother-in-law to Annie Russell. Her pleasant home is at the extreme end of this central peninsular, just beyond our view from this position, but plainly in view as one approaches or leaves this place by water, an account of which has been given on a previous page.

On turning back to take another view up the Pemaquid river, as far as we can discern it from the castle, we can see a one story farm house occupied by Mr. John Blaisdell and a family of his relatives. Two large barns are also visible and a small portion of the fine farm connected, which comprises a tract of land which the waters of this river nearly surround, forming a fertile peninsular. This was the former home of Col. Thomas Brackett, who was my great grandfather. His daughter Elizabeth, my grandmother, called Aunt Betsey, was born there. Col. Brackett came here from Boston a short time previous to the Revolution. I have been told that he was rather a wild boy there with his brothers, and his father purchased that farm and gave it to him that he might be removed from the temptations of the city. He became quite prominent in the town, and after being appointed an officer, was authorized to visit Worcester, Mass., to obtain ammunition for his Company to use during the war. After the war he had a vessel which he used for traffic between this place and Boston. It is related that the farmers' crops nearly failed them here one season, and he having good credit at Boston obtained much grain and other goods of John Hancock, and trusted them to many of the towns people who could never pay him. His farm was mortgaged to secure the debt, yet his creditors let him occupy it as long as he lived. Afterwards John Hancock failed, although his father is said to have left him $75,000. An incident that occurred on board of his vessel when lying in this harbor serves to show us that there were slaves held here at that time, quite a number of whose descendants still reside here. The last name given them was that of their owners. Jack Brackett was the name of the one whom my ancestor owned.

This story was told me when a small child by my grandmother. One day her only brother named Thomas was on board the vessel in the harbor with the slave, who was employed in the cabin below deck. He missed the noise of the boy on deck and going up was surprised to find him missing. He knew that he must be overboard and lost no time in going after him. He succeeded in his efforts in finding him and restoring him, although he had nearly perished. My grandmother informed me that ever after when her father visited Boston he would never bring home anything for his son, not even a pocket-handkerchief, without bringing the same thing for the slave.

As I remember my grandmother she was a jolly little woman. She married Jacob Partridge, who once was a boon companion of the Indians then living here, and with others attended their dances and other amusements, but finally joined a society of Friends, or Quakers, who had a small Meeting in the upper part of the town, now set off and called Bremen.

Old Fort House, Barn, and Tablet Inscribed: "A Large Number of Cannon Balls Fell in This Vicinity."

Looking West from Fort House, Showing Cellars of the Officers' Houses and One Side of Land Occupied by the Fort, with Rock Enclosed at [illegible]er

He afterwards moved to the town of Whitefield, Maine, which was seventeen miles from the nearest Quaker Church, yet he was so devoted a member that he used to walk there Sundays and Thursdays to attend their service, until able to procure a horse. He then moved to the town of Winslow, fifty miles from here. They raised a large family of boys and girls, part of which joined the society of Friends. James, one of the youngest, finally came into possession of this historic place, on which the fort was located. He presented it to the Monumental Association for the historical benefit of our estate. This society being too small to accomplish the work desired, turned the property over to the State, and three Commissioners were chosen by the Governor to care for it. Mr. Partridge being a brother of my mother I sought this place of refuge when my health failed me, and with the kind care of my relatives gradually recovered, and have devoted a good portion of the past twenty-five years to investigation of the history of this once noted locality.

When about six years of age, my grandmother one day was telling me about the old Fort; stories that she had heard when a child living there. Said she:—

"My mother learned to write on birch bark when confined there in the Fort from fear of the Indians."

Of course pens, ink and paper, were not to be had as readily as now, and I found when reclapboarding the old house a few years ago, that the builders had used this same material placed in strips, one overlaping the other, all up and down the seams of the plank with which the house is covered instead of boards, as building is done today. She spoke of cannon balls and bomb shells, and when I inquired of her what a bomb shell was, she gave this answer: "A bomb shell is round like a cannon ball, made of iron, and hollow inside, which they fill with powder, then fire them up over your house and they crush down through the roof and tear things all to pieces when they explode." I judge she must have heard the stories of the people confined in the Fort when De Iberville captured it. For more than fifty years I learned no more of Pemaquid, and had no further interest there until recently.

After the efforts of over twenty years we have interested enough people, so that we have succeeded in getting a small appropriation from the state sufficient to restore the Castle about the Old Rock at the West corner of the Fort. As we could not expect to obtain funds of the state sufficient to restore the whole original structure, we deemed this the wisest plan to have the Castle restored, which forms a Monument and Museum, making a suitable place to preserve and exhibit the many relics gathered in this vicinity, also the Paintings, Engravings, Books, &c. which we have been gathering for several years, and had been exhibiting in small temporary buildings close about the Old Rock. At last, during the summers of 1907 and 8, the present structure was rebuilt again for the third time, upon the original foundations, which standing eight feet high, were found to be in good condition. This work was done at the expense of about $6,000, by an appropriation of the State of Maine. This Castle is a conspicuous object seen by approach to this place, either by land or water, with its three flags when flowing out beautifully from the tops of their staffs high above the Castle, first the English, then the French, and above them both our Stars and Stripes.

The English Ensign is a present from Mrs. Annie (Russell) York, the actress, the French flag from Mr. Howland Pell of New York, a model of the white flag on which are to be seen the 15 Fleur de Lis, used at the date of the capture of this Fort in 1696 by De Iberville. The American flag was a present from our well known townsman Mr. Edward Drummond.

No visitor to ancient Pemaquid should fail to stand upon the restored Castle over the top of the Old Fort Rock, in close proximity to the steamer landings and the "Old Fort House," which is the best locality about here to obtain a fine panoramic view of the Pemaquid river, both harbors, the fields, bay, and

James W. Partridge and wife, Sarah, Owners and Occupants of the old Fort House and farm, from 1840 to Aug. 14, 1888; donors of the site of the Fort for the historic benefit of the State of Maine

ocean, also the site of the former settlements and Forts here and across the river. All the land to be seen from this Castle is a part of Pemaquid.

By a glance at the picture here shown with the bushes then about it, one can form an idea of how it appeared about the Rock in 1893, when we discovered the foundation of the old Castle which had been buried for 118 years, ever since the Revolution of the Americans against the English, when it was torn down to prevent them from using it against the inhabitants of this locality in 1775. The discovery that this wall of the Castle existed here, was made by finding a description of the Fort in 2nd Vol. Page 540, of Cotton Mathers writings, called the Magnolia. Many people knew that a fort once stood on this locality, but its foundation walls being covered entirely by the stone and crumbled mortar and dirt that had accumulated over them, so that no person living knew the form of the fort, or even the existence of the Castle wall.

By excavating about ten feet of this wall, as shown in the next view, we found 8 feet of the wall still standing, and so strong and so well laid, in a mortar, the composition of which is a puzzle to masons to-day, that the Castle has been restored on this foundation which did not have to be taken down, though it was built over two centuries ago. By continuing excavations we found 6 feet of the front wall of the fort still intact, which is about 150 feet long. This was "the Wall toward the sea," as described by Mather, 6 feet thick at the bottom and 22 feet high. We have now gotten all the foundations excavated and just enough restored so that people can walk all the way around the outlines of the fort and perceive that it covered about one half acre of ground. It is very plain to be seen how this foundation wall became covered so deep, the walls of the Castle being some three feet thick, the front wall thick and 22 feet high when the upper part was torn down the large mass of debris naturally fell against the foundation and kept accumulating till it formed a mound all along these walls, sloping off with an easy grade from thirty to fifty feet, so that people could easily walk up over the walls without mistrusting what was beneath their feet. They had been buried so long that the mortar on the surface had crumbled, dirt had accumulated, and with the growing vegetation had completely obscured the walls and debris from view, and it was fortunate they were thus saved, for by this we are able to prove that here once stood the strongest fort ever built by the English within what is now territory of the United States. These same stone are found to be the most convenient to restore the walls, which have been torn down twice.

The object in having this Castle restored was that we might have a suitable place to preserve and exhibit the many relics excavated about the fort, paintings and pictures pertaining to its History. By entering this Castle through the arched doorway on the east side, and proceeding up stairs, visitors will behold the most unique museum in this country. This second floor comes just to the top of the celebrated Rock of Pemaquid, over which is an opening, octagon in shape, about twelve feet across, showing the Rock, and from the great skylight above of the same size and shape, which admits light to this floor and the basement. Eight hard pine columns support the center of the roof leading up from each corner of the octagon angles. As one passes around the interior from left to right, first to be observed is a long hard pine table built on a curve to correspond with the sides of the Castle, on which are shown cases containing cannon balls found at the base of the front wall when it was unearthed, about 1890. Many souvenirs of the place and postal cards of historic interest are to be obtained. Next a fine large picture of one of the old Viking ships, such as crossed the ocean to these shores, in the year 1001. A portrait of Sir John Popham who sent the Popham colony to this place in 1607. Next is a large painting of Sir William Phips, who built this the third fort here of stone, which took nearly two thirds of the whole appropriation of the

State of Massachusetts for the year 1692. Phips was a remarkable man, a native of Maine, being born near Bath. He was the first American to be Knighted by the King of England, and the first American to be chosen Governor by him when the colonies of Plymouth and Massachusetts united. This portrait was painted by Miss Elizabeth Patterson of Wiscasset, Maine. The next is a painting of Sieur De Iberville, by the Artist Charles Huot, of Quebec, Canada. This man was the commander of the three men-of-war that captured Fort William Henry in 1696, four years after it was constructed. He dismantled it and took away the cannon, eight of which were brought from Portland by Phips. Portland was then called Falmouth. The French and Indians having killed all the inhabitants in 1690, leaving their bodies on the ground, where they remained until Phips visited the place two years later and finding their bones lying uncovered, buried them humanely, and took the cannon to Pemaquid. It is recorded in history, that the authorities of Massachusetts did not properly support or furnish soldiers to protect that region against their enemies in Fort Loyal at Portland. Those cannon were described by Mathews as eighteen pounders, which were the largest used on the fort, and with the carriages to move them about on the platform with, must have weighed a ton each. I judge by examining a gun that is mounted on the common at Bath, Maine, which was obtained from the British ship Samoset wrecked on Cape Cod during the Revolution. That cannon has the British mark of the broad Arrow on the top the same as the shot found here, that designates their make, the same as U. S. and other letters the make or ownership, of the nation to whom they belonged. By measuring I found the bore of the gun to be the same diameter as the large shot which we find here occasionally, by excavating about the Fort walls. Although the shot thrown by the French have been gathered in the field in range of the fort by the barrel and sold for old junk, we do not find but few of the British, for the self-evident reason that the two enemies when fighting exchanged their shot so that those fired from the fort must lay at the bottom of the ocean. When the French found that they could not capture this fort with the guns and small shot they had, which would fire about one mile, as proved by distance from Johns Island and Beaver behind which they lay to attack the fort, and where the shot have been found most plenty, in the fort field near the burying ground. They had not force enough to penetrate even one thickness of the six foot front wall, which they attempted to destroy. Meeting with no success on the first day, at night they established a battery on the heights of the shore across the river, and using a new missel of war, for those times, (the bomb shell) soon captured the fort. I think this is the first fortification taken by their use on this continent.

It seems that the English had no bomb shells or bomb proof covering for their protection, consequently when the French began to throw them over the walls of the Fort they were demoralized, the soldiers and all the people of the village being penned within these walls like a herd of cattle, and threatened with massacre by the two hundred Indians, who under Baron De Castine on shore, were assisting the French fleet. By the terms of surrender made they were to be escorted safely to the Islands, but if they continued to fight and were captured, then they were to be at the mercy of the Savages, who threatened to massacre them all. When we consider the advantage of the French at this time and the men, women and children of all the settlement gathered within these walls, I hardly wonder that the commander gave up the fort to save their lives, although he was severely critized for so doing. We next have a painting of the three ships used by De Iberville to capture the fort. They are queer looking old craft, resembling the Carovel that were sailed to this country by Columbus, with high quarter deck, and the bowsprit running into the air at an angle of forty-five degrees, requiring a sail to be used beneath them, called a water sail.

Gen. Joshua L. Chamberlain

Next we have a plan of Fort William Henry, which was obtained by Mr. James P. Baxter, from the public records of London a few years ago, which is very interesting, as we have found the foundation walls which we have excavated to correspond with it. Then we have a portrait of General William North, who was the first person born in the last fort restored here, about 1729 and re-named Fort Frederick. He became a soldier under Washington during the Revolution. Beneath these pictures is a show case containing many relics excavated from the ground inside the walls of the fort. Here also is an Airport Cover from the battleship Maine, which was sunk in Havana harbor in 1898. Passing on, we have the paintings of the fight between the Boxer and Enterprise, which occurred at Pemaquid during the war of 1812, and of the old schooner Polly, said to be the oldest one in America, having been built in 1805. These were painted by a local artist, as well as one of the old style Pinkey Susan, the Constitution and the convict ship Success, a wonderful old craft, built of Teak wood, and one hundred and twenty-six years old, once used as a prison ship at Australia by the British. Ex-Governor Fernald's portrait. Ex-Gov. Gen. Joshua L. Chamberlain, is remembered as a person who when Commissioner of this place understood well the importance of it, and we regretted that he had to retire. A fine portrait of our friend T. J. Oakley Rhinelander of New York, who for the interest he has in our history, makes us a yearly contribution. Two more very interesting pictures are of the former owners of the old Fort, Capt. John Nichols and his wife, and others who have become interested in this place.

Below these paintings and pictures above described, are large show cases well filled with many rare relics found about the old Fort and gathered in the town and state during the past twenty-five years. They consist of swords, guns, bayonets, cannon balls, bomb shells and fragments, bullets, piece of sail from the Enterprise that was in the battle off

Pemaquid in 1813, old tin lantern, used without glass, ancient buttons, old iron knives and forks, pewter implements, hoes, a one pronged pick axe, old hammers, and a variety of Indian implements. I have found former camping grounds of Indians in a dozen places about here. We also have a small collection of books pertaining to Maine history. Around the octagon opening, before described, is first a show case with a small but rare collection of relics from two other fortifications near by, one of them in full view from this place on the opposite bank of the river, which I will describe later. An old red cradle is an object of interest, a tin baker for use by the old fireplaces, old baking oven door, flat irons and andirons, bear trap over one hundred years old. Frows, once used to split shingles when they were made to last, also for splitting out the Tree-nails to use in securing the planks to vessels. One small cannon, supposed to be of Spanish make. We have two relics from the ocean, one from the waters of Pemaquid, the other from the eastern shores of Maine; two of the largest lobsters ever exhibited in New England, forty-four inches in length and weighing, one 25 the other 26 pounds when caught. Many freak lobsters are on exhibition, and numerous fresh water lobsters from brooks at North Carolina, which but few people seem to know anything about, though there are many in this state. We have hundreds more relics, too numerous to mention, which are not on exhibition, because we have not yet been able to secure the show cases to put them in. Now by ascending another flight of stairs, visitors can have a splendid panoramic view of uncommon interest from the top of the Castle.

In the basement people can walk all around the great Rock upon the cement floor and paving of the Magazine located at the north end of the Rock and partly covered by its projection at the top, thus forming a partial bomb-proof cover for it, according to the French account, (we have to get both the French and English account for much information of Pemaquid) the English kept their ammunition and guns in this Magazine which was nicely paved with small cobble stones similar to those of a part of the paving of the streets. Many relics gathered about the fort and vicinity are shown about this Rock, on which is the conspicuous date of 1607, to commemorate the important event of the first landing of the English people at this place, 13 years previous to the landing of the Pilgrims at Plymouth.

The great square mansion called the "Old Fort House," crowns the highest part of the peninsula. As we gaze from our positions on the top of the Castle or from the decks of steamers entering the harbor, it is the most conspicuous object upon it, except the stone Castle.

Between this Castle and village, looms up the Jamestown Hotel. At the east end of the peninsula a rough stone wall encloses a part of what Mrs. Hackelton in her poem calls "a field of graves." A few years ago a large canning factory was located on the west side of this peninsula. Many depressions are seen here and there where cellars have not been entirely filled up, also nearly a level field some twenty or thirty feet above high water mark, sloping every way to its water boundary.

On this peninsula which was once the busy metropolis of New England, I have been able to trace about forty of the three hundred walled cellars which were said to have been counted here in 1835. Here near the mouth of this river, by our Rock of Pemaquid, is the spot where Capts. Popham and Gilbert landed with fifty of their people, August 10th, 1607; there they were met by Nahanada, who had been taken to England by Capt. Geo. Waymouth in 1605, the chieftain of this place, with one hundred of his dusky warriors with drawn bows and arrows, who welcomed them to this country.

To find out when that old mansion was built, has been one of my puzzles about this place for the last decade. Soon after coming to Pemaquid in 1888, a lady named Mrs. Mahala Paul, nearly ninety years of age, then visiting here from Boston, who was born at Pemaquid Point, informed me that it was built by Col. David Dunbar. By referring to Prof. Johnson's history, I find that Dunbar came here in 1729 to rebuild Fort Frederick on the foundation of Fort William Henry, the first stone fort here erected by Phips. If her account is correct, the old house would now be about one hundred and eighty-five years old.

I am indebted to Mr. James H. Varney, Register of Deeds at Wiscasset, Maine, for much valuable information concerning this place.

From the Probate Records of Lincoln County, Maine, 1760–1800, V. 18, P. 169.

In the name of GOD amen. I Alexander Nickols of Bristol in the County of Lincoln Esquire, considering the uncertainty of this mortal life, and being of sound and perfect mind, blessed be almighty GOD for the same. Do make and publish this my last Will and testament in manner and form following that is to say, First.— * * * * * *

Then follows details of property willed to his wife and other members of his family, and to his youngest son the following:

I also give and bequeath to my youngest son John and his Heirs and Assigns All that my Mansion house, barn, buildings, and tenements situate lying and being at Pemaquid Old Fort, in Bristol afore said, with all my other lands in lots or parcels situate lying and being there at or there abouts. * * * * * *

Witness { Sallie Simenton
Ezra Poland
Robert McLintock

Probated 2 July, 1799.

From Capt. Thomas Nichols and his sister Deborah Morton, of Round Pond, I have gained much information about the old house and its occupants. Capt. John Nichols and family occupied the place till about 1840. He was the grandson of Capt. Alexander Nichols, who held a lieutenant's commission and was sent to command Fort Frederic about 1750, and is supposed to have been the last commander of the forts here.

Capt. John Nichols, Former Owner of Old Fort House

Alexander Jr., commanded a militia company during the time of the French and Indian war; after the war was over [1759] he settled at Pemaquid, and by the above will conveyed the old mansion to Capt. John, which brings its history down where we can trace it to date.

Capt. Nichols informed me that the old house was not square originally; the front was the same shape as now, extending back about two-thirds the present size, which can be seen by the sills and foundations of the original chimneys, one of solid stone, the other containing a great archway, such as were used by the farmers many years ago for storing vegetables during the winter time. Four great fireplaces, which consumed an abundance of wood, supplied heat for cooking and comfort for all its inmates during the winter time.

This house has been changed over so much, both inside and out, that it now presents little of its former appearance. The two original chimneys were taken down about 1860, leaving space enough for four good sized rooms on the two stories where they with their fireplaces, ovens, ashpits, etc., were located. New windows have taken the place of the old ones which formerly admitted light for the interior, through green tinted seven by nine panes of glass. The old substantial blinds are gone, the fancy caps and fluted casings that once ornamented the doorways have given place to plainer finish.

Relic hunters began the change on the outside some years ago by pulling out many of the hand-made nails which secured the weather-beaten, rift and scarfed clapboards to the upright planking, and they had to be replaced with new modern clapboards and nails.

When it was repaired a few years ago, it was found that planks one and one-half inches thick were used instead of boards to cover the walls, and were secured with hand-made spikes to the solid frame; they were placed upright instead of horizontal as to-day; every seam was covered with wide strips of birch bark instead of prepared paper as used now. The space between the boarding and planking was found to be filled with brick and mortar, no doubt to prevent the bullets of the Indians from penetrating the walls.

Capt. Nichols drew for me a plan of a long rambling ell which once led off at a right angle with the main house, toward the barn facing to the southwest, and was conveniently divided into small rooms such as were required at that time. First a pantry or milk room, then a wood shed, next a carriage house, house and a room for the pigs.

Capt. Nichols fell in love with a fair damsel who resided there when he was young, and his eyes brightened with pleasure as he related the story of many happy days and evenings passed with her by the open fireside of the old mansion and of the jolly sleighing parties they enjoyed in winter when they had no occasion to return home at an early hour. She owned the odd name of Zuba Blake, but afterward consented to have it changed to Nichols.

The next owner of the old house was Mr. Samuel P. Blaisdell, who came into possession of it about 1840, and carried on the occupation of farming. He was an uncle of Mr. Calvin C. Robbins, now of Bristol Mills, but who formerly resided here. I am indebted to him for much valuable and authentic information about the old fort foundations, pavings, cannon ball, and other relics to be mentioned in another chapter.

Col. James Erskine of Bristol Mills, purchased the old homestead of Mr. Blaisdell about 1845, but never came here to reside. He sold it to Mr. James W. Partridge, who moved here from the upper part of the town on January 11, 1847. There was then only one other house in sight, and the old mansion had the reputation of being haunted. The farm then included, with the Fort field and site of the old settlement, over four hundred acres, that part on Pemaquid Point being covered with a fine growth of wood, principally spruce.

Mr. Partridge and wife Sarah S. (formerly Erskine) occupied the place till his death on August 14, 1888. They reared a

Mrs. Capt. John Nichols

large and honorable family, three of whom reside here and three who have sought a home and business elsewhere. Their oldest boy, Eben H., died when quite young, and the oldest daughter, Jennie E., who was the beloved wife of Mr. Nathan George Lewis of this place, died June 11, 1895. She had the honor of being the first postmistress of Pemaquid Beach, and received the respect and confidence of all who knew her.

Hundreds of pleasant stories are connected with that old home, while the domicile of the Partridge family, and hundreds of people can say, "beneath that roof I have passed some of the happiest days of my life." It has sheltered more people than live in sight of it to-day, the white man, the Indian who slept wrapped up in his blanket on the brick hearth by its open fireplace, and the Negro slaves of its early owners. Beneath that roof have been enjoyed the fond lovers' courtships, the wedding ceremony, the happy days of the "honeymoon" with song, dance and music, and oft the gayest lads and lassies gathered there for social parties and made the old walls ring with echoes of their joy and mirth. Many a child first saw the light of day within those walls, and there with the last sad rites to mortals given, has been sung the sad refrain, which was sung there at the funeral of Mr. James W. Partridge.

We'll never say good-bye in Heaven,
We'll never say good-bye,
For in that land of joy and song,
We'll never say good-bye.

A story will illustrate the generosity of Mr. Partridge and his family of whom it used to be said, "they seem to run a free hotel there." A few years ago the fine little steam yacht Carita, owned by Mr. Alfred Davenport of Boston, brought here a party of his friends from Squirrel Island to look over the old ruins. As a part of them stood near the old house, one of our citizens, Mr. Myrick H. Marson, while speaking to them of Mr. Partridge, said: "I came here on one occasion to transact some business with him. I called him to the door and informed him of my business, but he would not listen to me till after dinner, urging me to come in and eat with the rest. From the door I could see a large company sitting at the table and I said, 'I do not want to go in there and eat with all those strangers, I don't know any of them.' 'Oh, never mind that,' Mr. Partridge said, '*I don't know them myself.*' "

I have heard "uncle Jim," as he was often called, say, "I never begrudged a person a meal of victuals in my life," and I never heard his wife or daughters complain about the extra amount of work they must have been obliged to do for all their company. With all their generosity and kindness to others, they have always had an abundance, and none of the family have ever suffered for lack of food, clothing, fuel, or any of the necessities of life.

I remember on one occasion Capt. Mellvin from Massachusetts, who used to reside here, came to the old house with his newly wedded bride to enjoy their "honeymoon" and there met many other visitors who used to come from Vassalboro and other towns back in the country to stop a few weeks by the seashore. Twenty-five people found food and shelter there on that occasion, and from "morn till eve" their song and laughter made the old house ring with pleasant echoes. Sailing and fishing parties were enjoyed down the bay by most of the company on pleasant days, which were often extended far into the night. The little drag boat, called the "Come On," owned by the author's brother, Jacob Alonzo, having a fine cabin, was a favorite with the young people then.

"Uncle Jim" had five sons then living, and two daughters, who by their good graces soon attracted the sons of other men and it was a singular coincidence that the oldest daughter, Jennie E., whose father owned the site of old forts on this side of the Pemaquid River, should select from her many suitors, Mr. George N. Lewis, the son of Mr. Nathan Lewis, who owned the site of the other fort and settlement across the river, even the name of which no one knows to-day.

Mr. Lewis used to come across on his regular visits to the old mansion in a small skiff, (he was a small man himself) which served him better than a horse and buggy to drive around by land. One night some mischievous boys played a trick on him by hauling his "team," as they called it, up from the river bank where he had left it to return home as usual, when his visit was ended. They took it in through the back door to the kitchen, tied it to the door latch and piled up in front of it a generous supply of good hay. When George returned to the shore during the small hours of the night, he was surprised to find that his skiff had vanished. He was obliged to return and remain at the old mansion till morning. But he, being a good natured lad, full of fun and mischief and fond of playing tricks upon other people, could not well complain of this one which had been played upon himself.

A jolly, roving lad named Asa Johnson Dodge, captured Mr. Partridge's youngest daughter Clara. He used to drive a team called a "Peddler Cart," dispensing dry goods and Yankee notions to the people all over the town of Bristol. After marriage they settled down at Pemaquid Falls, where he carried on a thriving business with a store from which you could obtain all kinds of goods, from a pump tack to a bag of grain. He became town treasurer, often presided at town meetings, served his townsmen as representative to the legislature, was postmaster several years till about 1897, being assisted by his wife and family.

Pemaquid being too small for his growing ambition he removed his family, consisting of Mrs. Dodge, three daughters and two sons, to Roxbury, to swell the population of Massachusetts, which has absorbed so many of our good citizens, to be regretted by their friends remaining here.

A Remarkable Duck Story.

A story now occurs to me that has connection with the old barn as well as an inmate of the old house; it is a tough duck story, but having heard it from the lips of Mr. Partridge and his two daughters, Jennie and Clara, I cannot doubt their words or those of many other witnesses still living, who are willing to testify to the truth of the circumstances here related.

Some twenty years ago Mr. Partridge had a small flock of eight ducks which he delegated to the care of Miss Clara, giving her the proceeds of their daily supply of eggs. She soon found that she was getting each day one more egg than there were ducks, which at first puzzled her very much. The ducks were not liberated from their pen in the old barn, until they had laid in the morning, and to find out which one laid the double quantity, they shut them up separately until the right one was found. This was soon accomplished; and that duck became a pet, and her fame was known for fifty miles around. This noble bird kept up her profitable occupation through the whole summer season, and the next year she beat her own record by laying *three eggs per day*. They always used to let her out after she had laid two eggs, but one day they discovered a nest full of duck's eggs in a bed of tansy just south of the old barnyard wall, and soon found that she was laying two eggs for Miss Clara and one for herself. This Mr. Henry Partridge now tells me they proved by keeping her shut up in her cage, made of boards and laths, till they secured all she laid.

After listening to this story, which all three of the sons now residing here verify, Mr. James Partridge adds, " I also have heard father say to people to whom he told the story, 'If you don't believe me you can take that duck home with you and if she doesn't lay twenty-one eggs in seven days, I will give you one hundred dollars,' " and Mr. Fred A. Partridge adds to his brother's testimony, "Yes, and I have heard him say if she don't lay you twenty-one eggs in seven days you need not bring her back."

The loss of the whole flock occurred when the old barn was burned. Deacon Wm. Foster who came from Rockport, Mass., and used to keep a store here, and was for several years Superintendent of the Sabbath School at New Harbor, was one of the first at the fire, and he and Mrs. Partridge saw the flock apparently very much frightened by the fire, when they flew away across the river and were lost to view.

CHAPTER XVI.

THE OLD CELLARS OF PEMAQUID.

IN many places along the lines of buried paving and in other localities where we have not yet traced any paved streets, are depressions, generally with small mounds about them, which indicate by the difference in the vegetable growth upon them and their composition, that they are composed of soil thrown up from beneath the original surface.

There are certain seasons of the year when these cellars can be seen to better advantage; if you look for them after the grass has grown up quite tall you may see but little indications of their existence; but just after haying time, or in the spring when the snow has melted away upon the fields these depressions will remain filled with ice and snow for a long time, and can be readily distinguished in distinct rows for a long distance.

The only cellars remaining on this little peninsula which have not been partially filled up, except by rubbish, are two that lie just west of the old fort house, near the western walls inside of the boundary line of the old fort, where were located the houses of the officers. The walls of these cellars which have been exposed to the elements for more than a century, still show the effects of good workmanship; no better walls can be laid by any mason to-day with natural stone than in these cellars and others which I have examined. It is a well known fact to all stone-masons that walls of this kind must be properly laid to prevent the frost from tearing them to pieces in winter, after they have been exposed by the destruction of the building above.

Mr. John Stinson in his testimony read before the Maine Historical Society, informs us that he counted three hundred cellars here in 1835.

Mr. William Erskine when looking over the place with me a few years ago, said, "I have counted over seventy cellars on one street along that creek," pointing to the east side of the peninsula which is bounded by McCaffrey's creek.

Most of them have been so long cultivated over that they cannot be readily located now. According to Mr. Partridge's account the largest one of the depressions on this street was the cellar of Morgan McCaffrey for whom the creek was named (some claim it was called Cox's Cove previously) and whose gravestones attract much attention in the old burying ground. It is located about one-half way from the Hotel to the head of the creek. That with others along that shore has been filled up some since I came here.

A large bed of strawberries has been cultivated about the McCaffrey cellar; it was a convenient place to throw in stray weeds, turf and stone, and in that way the cellars are finally evened up with the surrounding fields until their locality cannot be discerned.

In 1888, Mr. Partridge once said to me, "I have filled up over forty of these cellars since I owned this place in about forty years."

Capt. J. B. Fitch who told me about the pavings, said, "along this main street were cellar walls thick enough, and heavy enough to support any block of buildings in the city. Your father (Elijah P. Cartland) helped me dig out one of several found on Fish Point when I built a wharf and store there, just before the civil war, and we found the bottom floored over with logs hewn on three sides and bedded nicely together in the soil. We found in one cellar some relics; one was a gun made before the flint-locks were. It had a flash-pan as large as a small saucer."

We have the evidence of many people who have helped to

fill the cellars here; sometimes using paving stones, sometimes stone from the old forts, and sometimes soil.

On Pemaquid Point, Rutherford's, Witch Island, on each side of John's Bay, on the banks of the Damariscotta, the John's and the Pemaquid rivers are hundreds of cellars, many of them overgrown and surrounded with a growth of large trees. Many choice relics have been excavated from some of these cellars, and no doubt thousands more remain, which will interest the antiquarian when brought to light. No one to-day can tell the story of the past that belonged with every one of them, but all I have known to be dug out have furnished evidence of the civilization of the former owners whose homes were once located above those lonely excavations.

Sidewalk and section of Street over 40 feet wide, showing depth of Soil accumulated over it. Pavings extending nearly one-half mile have been found here, with many stone walled Cellars beside them

CHAPTER XVII.

ANCIENT PAVINGS.

Green is the sod where, centuries ago,
  The pavements echoed with the thronging feet
Of busy crowds that hurried to and fro,
  And met and parted in the city street;
Here, where they lived, all holy thoughts revive,
  Of patient striving and of faith held fast;
Here, where they died, their buried records live;
  Silent they speak from out the shadowy past.

M. W. HACKELTON.

THE greatest mystery of all the relics found at old Pemaquid within the last century are her wonderful and extensive pavings, beyond the reach of any recorded history yet brought to light, as to their origin, and yet showing where the people have left them as originally laid, the best specimens of that kind of work done with natural stone that I have ever seen. The extent and workmanship which I have been able to examine a portion of, in three different localities, two on the east and one on the west side of the river, indicate the settlement of a people well advanced in civilization.

Having heard much about the paved streets before I commenced investigations here, I have taken much pains to obtain correct information concerning the history as far back as possible, and with the time and means at my disposal, to examine all that has been exposed during the last decade.

As soon as my health would permit after coming here, I began excavations and work on a cottage to cover the pavings and preserve the relics found. Mr. Partridge kindly showed me a convenient spot and gave me the free use of it. "But" said he, speaking from his past experience, "it will be no use for you to uncover it unless you can protect it with a building for the relic hunters will carry away every stone you uncover unless you protect them."

I did not have the funds to pay for a very elaborate building; but after some delay put up a structure 12 x 15 feet, and one story, using the paving for the floor and on shelves placed relics and curiosities that were gathered here, forming a sort of a museum and named it the "Paving Cottage." I could only exhibit a small piece some 10 x 12 feet square, as the platform on which people stood to view it with rail in front to keep them from going on to it, covered a part from view.

This was not satisfactory to me or all of my visitors, rather a small exhibit where so much had been claimed and some would naturally say, "Well they might have laid that some time in the night to have it to exhibit." But I knew that there was more of it joining what I had on exhibition, for by having a narrow trench dug at right angles from the fine cobble-stones toward the fort foundations, I found paving extending that way thirty-three feet, with a good water course and curbstone on the outer edges. This was of flat stones filled in with some cobbles from the shore to make it all compact.

I finally got permission of the heirs of Mr. Partridge, he having died in 1888, to uncover more of the paving, and I then had the building moved to the northern edge of it and enclosed it with a fence, and having a raised platform over part of it. This gives visitors a good opportunity to view and examine both kinds of stone work. So we have now on exhibition what appears to be a short section of a street about ten feet above high water mark, leading down a fine, easy sloping field toward a small sand beach, an inbent line of the harbor shore, a pretty place to bathe, and where the children love to play and build forts of the fine white sand, in summer.

The larger stones form what we term the main street, which

is thirty-three feet in width, including the gutters, or water courses. The finer work of cobble-stones evidently taken from the beach near by is eleven and one-half feet wide. The longer cobbles were selected and placed across the sidewalk on lines two feet and one-half apart, then the space filled in with smaller ones. One row is laid diagonally, as if to form the corner of a square yard, and it might have been thus fancifully done because it was the front yard paving of some former mansion; no prettier place could have been found along the shore, and it was in close proximity to the fort. The other part we found to be laid in sections, when we got it swept off, for no one can see the fine workmanship until the seams are cleared of soil and all swept off, because the uneven stones could not be laid level like flat ones. Unobserving people would pass over that exposed by the plough because the plough can go no lower than the tops of the highest stones, leaving all others entirely covered with soil.

All this was done systematically, for I found by measurements that the larger paving sloped from the center either way to the gutters, which are nicely laid with selected stone for the curbing and finer cobbles for the center, all compactly placed, and serving to drain both parts of the pavings, which were found to be twelve inches beneath the soil at the center, and fifteen at the edges. That is not a great depth compared with volcanic burials of ancient streets, or in localities that have the wash of running water; but for this locality it seems deep, being on a nearly level field, and in other places on the very highest part of the peninsula.

At first I thought it might have been caused by decayed vegetable matter which had, year by year for centuries, accumulated there, but I gave up that theory when I found it was covered with rich soil well mixed with course and fine gravel. It is now thought to be the work of angle or earth worms, and that theory has some foundation from the fact that every spring and fall they throw up the soil between the cobbles so that we have frequently to sweep it up and take it away to prevent the stones from being completely hidden from view.

This corresponds with experiments made by Prof. Darwin some years ago with a piece of board, which he laid flat on the soil in his garden; the worms soon covered it from view with soil which they brought to the surface. Few people can realize the amount of work those little earth worms can do unless they study their habits.

Mr. Partridge's Evidence.

As we walked up the field from the shore where the cottage now stands, Mr. Partridge said, "I have traced the paving up through this field by ploughing and digging to the road; and from there on to where the gates of the forts were located in front of the old house, then out to the burying-ground. I have tried several times to plough them out, but found them so large that the only way to get rid of them was to dig them up and haul them away. Some years ago a gentleman from Bangor, Maine, came here and stopped several weeks, making surveys and a plan of the pavings found here. He was an invalid and I used to have to help him out of bed in the morning." I could not get any information about this person or the results of his work, as Mr. Partridge had forgotten his name.

J. Reed Partridge, a brother of the above named James, now residing at Bremen, went over this field with me and pointed out the locality of the main street as he saw it when he helped his brother to plough up the field many years ago.

Capt. Lorenzo D. McLain's Evidence.

He is a boat builder, and has resided at the Beach many years. One day, about three years ago, he surprised me by bounding in through the doorway of the Paving Cottage, and with a pleasant salutation said, as he made a solid landing on the platform with both feet at once, "There! this is the first time I have ever been inside of this building since you put it up."

After examining the relics and pavings he gave me the following information: "When I was a small boy, about 1855 I think it was, I helped your uncle Jim plough this field. He had got a new No. 8 plough and was going to plough his land deeper than he had been doing. He had Capt. Alfred Bradley (still living) and Willard Jones with two yoke of oxen, and my job was to hold down the plough beam and keep it clear.

"Every time we came 'round on this side of the field the plough would come up some ways in spite of all we could do, and it appeared to slide along on something like a ledge, but we could not think a ledge would be so even.

"At last he got out of patience and turning to me said, 'Jemes rice,' that was his worst swear expression; 'boy, go up to the barn and get a hoe and the crowbar, and we will see what there is here.' Then we found this paving, and where we first cleared it off it seemed to be laid in cement; and we had to dig a long time with the crowbar before we could get out the first stone."

When we uncovered the larger stone paving I found it had the appearance of having been disturbed on the part now covered by the platform. I inquired of Capt. McLain about that. "Oh!" said he, "that is the work of the relic hunters. When uncle Jim first found this he opened quite a piece and left it uncovered. One day I came along here and found that the relic hunters had dug out the smaller stones and taken them away; then uncle Jim had to cover it up to save it."

By examining the soil where the stone had been taken out, I found brick, charcoal, and other indications that the paving had been laid over ruins of some former structure, as I have before found relics beneath stone-work that showed plainly that the last structure was erected over the ruins of some previous one. This goes to prove the history of the place, stating that it has been repeatedly built up and destroyed. Mrs. Everett Lewis told me of indications of cellars, a fire-place, etc., found alongside this paving many years ago.

David Chamberlain, Esq., of this town, an aged gentleman then residing at Round Pond, Maine, pointed out a spot near the road and on a line with the paving now uncovered, where he uncovered a portion of the cobbles in 1869, to exhibit to the Members of the Maine Historical Society. Said he, "I uncovered a piece there in the morning thirty feet long and before night every stone was taken away."

Capt. Joseph B. Fitch of Chicago, who used to trade here, visited the place a few years ago and kindly went with me over the old paved streets leading out to the burying-ground, and pointed out the spots where, when a boy, he used to pick raspberries from bushes that grew up beside the curbstones of the street, which were afterward hauled away to the river bank.

Mr. Nathan Goold of Portland informed me that he visited Pemaquid about twenty-five years ago, and Capt. Patrick Tukey showed him pavings on that street and also between the cellars. Said he, "I think those people must have been *paving cranks*, to have paved their streets and between their houses too."

In the testimony given by Mr. Henry Varley in the account of the celebration given here in 1871, there were three points left unsatisfactory to me, in his statement that, "I was engaged with other men more than one week in digging up the pavement of one street."

That account failed to *locate* the street, give the *number* of men employed, or tell what they *did* with the paving stone. One day Capt. Patrick Tukey of Long Cove, came here to look over the ruins with me, and when standing upon the old Rock and gazing over the field he remarked, "I used to work on this place many years ago for Capt. Nichols."

I inquired "Did you ever see any one digging up any of the

paved streets here?" "Oh! yes I remember that Mr. Varley dug up one that ran from the shore to the burying-ground."

"How many men did he have employed with him?"

"Well, I can't just remember, but *three* or *four* I should say."

"What did they do with the stone, Captain?"

"Well, they had a cart and oxen, and after they dug them up with their pickaxes and crowbars they put them in the cart and hauled them to the shore and dumped them over the bank."

I was pleased to obtain this statement because it gave more definite information and confirmed my idea that it must have been a street with a steep grade where the soil had not gathered over it sufficiently deep to admit of cultivation without reaching it.

I have heard it said that the first indications of paving seen by recent settlers was on a field of grain where, during a drought, that above the paving suffered most, and being stunted, plainly marked its outline. By that means we are able to plainly trace all the buried walls of the fort, and the cellars can be traced with much more accuracy when the grass is short in spring or soon after being mowed over.

Mr. John Blaisdell who now resides near here on the old Col. Brackett estate, once showed me where Mr. Partridge ploughed over a cross street leading down from the main street toward the river, perhaps two-thirds of the distance from the old barn to the burying-ground. "I was driving the cattle," said he, "and the plough struck the edge of a flat stone and turned it out from among the rest, and uncle Jim made me stop the cattle, and he went back and put the stone in its place again."

About three years ago I had an opportunity to examine a portion of the main street pavings which were exposed well out toward the old cemetery, when the field was ploughed. It was in quite good condition, and paved with quite large cobbles.

Beside the many places where I have examined it, I have been shown another place where it was found on the bank of a small, sandy cove, near the present village, and close to the residence of Capt. George R. McLain and Llewellyn McLain. That found up the river, will come under an account of a trip to the Pemaquid Falls, three miles up this noted winding river.

I will close this chapter by a quotation from the report of the Maine Historical Society, of August 25 and 26, 1869, by the Secretary, Mr. Edward Ballard:

> By the diligence of some members of the local committee, a portion of the paved street had been laid bare by the removal of the superincumbent soil, to the depth of eight to eighteen inches, over which the ploughshare had often been driven in former years. The regular arrangement of the beach-stones, the depression for the water course to the shore, the curbstones, the adjoining foundation-stones still in place, articles of household furniture and implements of the artisan, all these and other concurring facts proved, beyond the possibility of a doubt, that a European community had dwelt on this spot, and had made this long street in imitation of what they had left in the mother land.

CHAPTER XVIII.

The Old Cache.

THIS word is derived from the French and is pronounced as though it was spelled *casha.* The definition as given in Webster's Dictionary, is a hole in the ground for hiding provisions which it is inconvenient to carry. They are quite common in our Western States now, and are used for hiding and preserving provisions, etc. The one found here was called a cistern, because no one knew its proper name or what it was built for. For many years after its discovery the structure remained an attractive relic, and a puzzle to all who examined it, until it vanished, brick by brick, like many of the other choice relics that have been excavated here.

This cache was different from any other I have ever learned of in our country, being walled up with odd shaped bricks, trapezoidal in form, so that when placed side by side, they formed a circle, as ordinary bricks do a straight line, and they were laid in a mortar composed principally of clay. It was about ten feet deep and nearly seven in diameter; once entirely covered and hidden beneath the soil. It was located on the bank of the river a few rods northerly from the fort. When constructed, the builders must have dug a hole in the ground exactly as in digging a well, and then used those odd bricks to form a wall, arching them over at the top, some two feet below the surface of the soil, so as to leave a small hole only at the top, just large enough for a person to crawl down and back through, called a "manhole." The "manhole" was evidently covered with a flat stone, and then by covering the top and removing the surplus soil dug out, and putting back the turf, as is done when finishing a lawn, or banking with cut turf, the growing grass or other vegetation would soon hide all evidence of the structure, with its store of valuables, or food, well hidden from the enemies of the builders.

There must have been times when food was of more value than gold or silver to some of our early colonists, when the enemies of the early settlers had attacked them, and plundered all their provisions at the forts and settlements, and driven the inhabitants to the islands. Of what use was money then? Where could they go to obtain food with it? Portland, Boston or New York did not exist; but when the enemy left, or when night came on, they could return in boats and secure their "staff of life." It seems to me that for some such emergency this structure was built, and it might have been used to hide other valuables beside. It took the old sailing vessels sometimes twelve weeks to cross the ocean, as we learn by the records of Richard Mather, concerning the James and Angel Gabriel. Without some such provision of surplus food they must have subsisted on the products of the ocean, the clam-flats and mussel-beds, or wild game, a long time, before they received food or supplies from across the Atlantic. I have found accounts of the early settlers that verify this statement of their food supply of clams, etc., upon which they had to subsist sometimes for many weeks.

The story of the discovery of this cache is as follows: Mrs. Mahala Paul, the old lady before mentioned in connection with the old fort house, and a relative, Miss Selina Upham, were walking along the bank of the river, which there forms the southern side of the inner harbor, and noticed some of those odd shaped bricks, which had fallen down to the water's edge, with the soil which had been undermined by the high tides and sea. (That work of the sea still goes on and I have noticed in the last decade, places where the soil has been washed away, back five feet or more.) They traced the bricks to their source near the top of the bank, and there beheld the whole circle of the structure outlined with those bricks, showing where the bank, when it slid down, took off the top of the cache. The storms had washed off soil from above, and completely filled the structure.

The ladies hastened to the house, and found the people just eating dinner; considerable excitement was manifested on the recital of their discovery, and those at dinner stopped eating and repaired to the cache, the men carrying tools to dig with. Mr. James W. Partridge, Elijah P. Cartland, George N. Lewis and Alonzo Partridge, were the men who dug it out, but they were disappointed; empty was the structure, and its treasures gone. Several years after coming here, we had a heavy storm, driving the water of the Bay further up than usual, and undermining the bank where this structure was, and exposing quite a piece of it still standing, which I was glad to see, and took pains to immediately protect it from further exposure by the sea, and from the relic hunters. I have since built a sea wall about 100 feet long, reaching out by it, which will protect it, I trust, until we can obtain funds to restore it.

This structure ought to be rebuilt as a monument of past history. It was a great misfortune to have it partially destroyed. We have collected many of the bricks that have been carried away in times past, giving each one credit for those returned, and we hope to receive many more. It would cost but a few hundred dollars to rebuild it, and it could be left partially uncovered for inspection. The Pemaquid Improvement Association will be glad to restore it as soon as they can obtain the money for that purpose.

The following letter sent me by Capt. Loring Fossett, a well known sea captain of this town, will throw much light on this antique structure.

"PEMAQUID, MAINE, Aug. 30, 1890.

"MR. J. H. CARTLAND,

"*Dear Sir :* — Your favor of yesterday's date, at hand this

A. M., and noted. So, to be as brief as possible, would say that I saw the cistern or vault, which was discovered at or near the ruins of the Old Fort. It was in the spring or early summer; it was partly filled with water, and was protected by a board fence of two rails high. I have a very vivid recollection of its size and bricks, etc., and was much interested concerning it, but saw no one who could give me any satisfactory idea concerning its former use.

In 1870, I made a voyage to the Mediterranean, and while at Leghorn, Italy, saw by the Military Barracks, a plot of ground containing some four or five acres, that contained many such underground structures, used for storing grain or military supplies. I noticed them by seeing the soldiers opening them, and taking the grain out to dry, which was wheat, barley and peas. The size was about eight feet in diameter and twelve feet deep; they had two feet of earth over them, and were opened by removing a small quantity of earth over the 'manhole,' or opening, which was round in shape, about fifteen inches in diameter, and a stone cover, which fitted closely. Some had iron covers, which indicated that their stone predecessors had been broken, or otherwise unfitted for use. The bricks were deep red, and made for the purpose to which they were put. I made inquiries about their construction, and was informed that the old Military custom was to build those underground vaults for the purpose of storing supplies and valuables, which were always kept in secret places near their strongholds.

The city of Leghorn having grown extensively in later years, of course has changed the topography of the surroundings of those particular Military posts of which I am writing, from their former appearance.

At the time I saw them, they were on a plot of ground about eight feet higher than the surrounding streets, walled up on all sides, and slightly crowning on top, enough to turn the water. In regard to the mortar of which they were constructed, I can give no idea, as the inside showed dingy from age and use. They entered them by a small rope ladder, and removed the grain with cloth bags, attached to a bow of wood, similar to our fish dip nets.

After removing the grain they were swept clean, dried, and the grain put back and covered as before. When removing the earth on opening them, the sod was cut clean and nicely removed, and when put back in its place, would take an expert to tell where they were. This custom, I was informed, was common in Italy in the middle ages and was very old. I have forgotten what they were called, but any Italian scholar can give you that information. I have never heard of any other nation using this custom. In haste, I am

Yours respectfully,

"L. H. Fossett."

CHAPTER XIX.

Remains of Blacksmith Shops.

IN former days, the music of the smithy's anvil rang through every village in the land, from morn till dewy eve, when nearly all iron implements were made by blacksmiths. I have often heard it said that there were seven blacksmith shops belonging to this place. Thus far I have only located the remains of two to my satisfaction; one upon Fish Point, said to have had two forges, one having a stone anvil, which Capt. L. D. McLain recently informed me he had used to cut off bolts when at work there. Said he, "When I dug out the cellar for that house," pointing out the one now occupied by Capt. Geo. R. McLain and family, "I found the remains of a blacksmith's shop there. I ought to know what belongs about them, for I have worked in them enough to learn. I found pieces of iron, slag, a cannon ball and a fragment of the end of a large cannon."

I have found on an old map several places marked along the shore north of the house above alluded to, where other shops were located. On the southerly side of the main street, leading from the fort to the burying-ground, a place has been pointed out as the former location of the "Village Square," where several blacksmith shops once existed. The remains of those most essential and common places of mechanical industry, like the carpenters' and shipbuilders' establishments, are now hard to trace; but all over this locality we find the relics of the smith's handiwork, ranging from a "Nigger hoe" to a ship-carpenter's pod-auger. Spikes, nails, knives, shears, cleavers, and a hundred other implements, were then worked out by hand, that now are made of cast iron and by machinery. The excellent material used, and the remains of fine work still plainly to be seen on the knives, shears, and some of the best-preserved implements found, indicate that if these were not imported articles, there were expert workers of iron here long ago. The iron used at that time was far superior to much of that manufactured to-day, as is shown by its resistance to the elements, and did not rust so readily.

CHAPTER XX.

Evidence of Pipe Making.

FOR many years past the old settlers of this place have often been known to speak of the "remains of pipe factories."

The second thing I dug for after coming here in 1888, was to find the foundation of one of those factories. On the western edge of an out-cropping ledge, between the hotel and outer harbor, I soon observed a mound about twenty feet in diameter, on which grew vegetation much more rank than that adjoining it. On digging a trench across it, I found the mound composed mostly of blue clay, like that of many of the natural deposits about here. A low stone wall partially divided the mound. On the edge the clay had turned red, indicating that it had been subjected to great heat, perhaps when the building above it was burned. At the edge of the mound I found a flat door bolt, hand-made nails, a lead bullet, etc. Among the clay and stones were charcoal, pipe bowls and stems, and on tipping over the lower stones more pipe fragments and relics, indicating that the last structure built there covered another of previous record, as found in other places, and by recorded history. I then replaced the stone and soil.

This was no thorough or satisfactory investigation, but it is better to leave what remains of this and many other historic spots, till we have time and funds to carefully excavate, preserve and make record of these footprints of the early settlers; then we shall be better able to read or trace their records along the pathway of time.

On the point of land just south of the Beach village, where

the main street leading to Fish Point intersects with the water at high tide, (where an ice-house used to stand till a few years ago,) is now a summer residence, — a fine cottage — of Mr. Josiah C. Evans of Vassalboro, Maine. Before either of those buildings were erected, indications of a large pipe factory were discovered, and many people used to dig out the fragments, and were sometimes rewarded by finding a whole pipe, or many bowls with short stems. Many have been found on the flats by excavations at low water, indicating that some of the fragments were thrown over the bank. Mr. Reed Partridge once stated to me that when he used to go over to Fish Point to plough up the land, he would run the plough along that ridge of land on his way, and it would turn out great quantities of pipe fragments.

All over this peninsula, when excavating pavings, fort walls, or even digging holes for posts, those fragments are found. Most of them are white, indicating the use of foreign clay. Some are red, and might have been made of the blue clay common here, which turns red on being subjected to great heat, or "burned," as people generally speak of finished bricks. I have succeeded in obatining only a few perfect pipes, but the odd shapes and sizes are interesting; the odd figures and letters found upon them, — even the stems being sometimes ornamented. On the bowls of many are pictures of human faces, ships, etc., but none with the "T. D." of modern make, which seems to show that they were the products of many different manufacturers. So few are alike, and the abundance found so widely scattered over this locality, indicates the general use of that poisonous plant called tobacco.

A tiny little pipe found at all three of the settlements in this vicinity, generally in and about the cellars and pavings, has attracted more attention than the larger ones, because it was so small one could not insert the tip end of the smallest finger in the bowl. I have recently learned that the proper name for them is the "Queen Mab" or "Irish Fairy" pipe. I have seen pictures of some from a collection by a New York gentleman, that were finely ornamented with pictures of faces on the side of the bowl. Some people have suggested that they might have been used to smoke opium in.

A party of Irish people once visited the Rock Cottage who were posted in Irish customs of their native land. While examining one of those little pipes, I inquired of one of the ladies if her people at home used such small pipes to smoke with. She answered with a hearty laugh, and said, "Oh ! no, those are not for the people to smoke at all, they are for the *fairies*. In our country in the west of Ireland, when the people used to have parties and festivals, they remembered the fairies, and formed a circle or small rings of grass in the field near where the festivities were held, and at night placed those little pipes around the rings for them to smoke."

CHAPTER XXI.

OLD VESSELS.

IT is well known to all people who obtain their livelihood about the salt water, that all the common wood of vessels, wharves, lobster traps, etc., is soon attacked by insects or worms, as they are generally called. One kind fairly honeycomb the plank and timbers of vessels with holes as large as pipe-stems, boring in all directions through the center of the wood, but like the cunning rats on board of ships, their instinct seems to teach them not to eat entirely through the outside of the planking, but leave just a thin shell on the outer surface.

No doubt many an old ship has been sunk by their means, for when the planks are thus eaten away, if the vessel strikes a floating log, timber, or ice-cake, as they are often likely to in the night, it would easily puncture a hole in the bottom that would soon cause them to fill with water and sink. Those larger worms are more troublesome in warm climates, and our larger vessels that frequent tropical ports are generally protected by large sheets of thin copper, firmly nailed on over all parts exposed to contact with the water. This process is called "sheathing," and is quite expensive.

Smaller vessels which can be readily hauled on some smooth beach at high water, when the tide leaves are easily rid of the barnacles, sea grass, and other parasites which grow upon them and obstruct their passage through the water. The sea-worms are destroyed and checked in their work of destruction, by frequent application of paint, some of which is very effectual.

Lobster traps are taken from the water frequently, and after remaining on shore a few weeks the worms die; they are then again ready for use, but the piling and logs of wharves, where they are constantly submerged, have to be replaced by new ones, as they are entirely eaten off in a few years.

These pests eat along the upright piling between the low water mark and the soil on the bottom of the river or harbor where the wharf stands, so they present a queer appearance: at low water we can often see piling a foot or more in diameter at the top, and near the bottom eaten away to the size of a person's wrist, leaving the hard knots which they do not fancy so well, projecting out in all directions. Below the soil the worms do not penetrate the wood, and that part remaining under soil and water protected from the air, will keep as perfect as when driven down, for centuries. I read of some removed at the old London Bridge, England, which were recently excavated, and found as perfect as when put down eight hundred years ago.

I have found several specimens of wood here which show the work of four different species of worms. The first honeycombs the wood, the second bores generally lengthwise of the wood and incases his hole as he goes along, with a beautiful white shell, about as thick as a sheet of writing paper, into which you can run an ordinary lead pencil with ease the whole length, it is so straight. Others bore in towards the heart of the wood, having their holes very thick together, and as smooth and neatly done as if made by the sharp tool of an artisan.

Another kind is a tiny little fellow about as long, though smaller round than the ordinary sea-flea, but very lively and he does the most mischief, eating altogether upon the outside of the wood. These facts will explain why we cannot be expected to find the remains of much pertaining to ancient wooden structures about here on the seashore.

I have only secured a few specimens that escaped the

ravages of the worms: one is a fine old quadrant, found under water a few years ago by Mr. Joseph Gifford of this place, when spearing bait for lobsters. This is composed of black ebony and must have been too tough for their teeth, for although so old that the metal attached to it is much corroded and some entirely gone, there are only a few pin holes in the wood to show any indications of the little wood destroyer.

Another specimen is a fragment of a ship's keel, about fifteen feet long, with rusty remnants of bolts, some over two feet long, projecting through it at short intervals, at right angles with the wood, indicating that it was part of the keel or keelson of a large vessel (possibly the Angel Gabriel before mentioned). What remains of this relic is completely saturated or petrified with the oxide of iron, and must have been what is termed the "heart" of the wood. Its hardness and the iron evidently saved it from destruction by the worms. This relic was brought to light by Mr. Pierce Munsey, by a lobster-warp that got wound about one end of it, and when pulling it up he broke it in two, leaving the remainder fast in the mud near the mouth of the river, where it was embedded.

There are several piles of stone to be seen along the banks of the Pemaquid River, among which, and beneath, are the timbers and other parts of vessels, some of which I can trace the history, and others date too far back to be traced. Those stone heaps, of such stone as we find about here, we understand are composed of the ballast of vessels, whose decaying timbers they now partially cover. When we find these heaps composed of *limestone* and *flint*, we infer the vessels carrying it were from foreign ports. I have never been able to learn of any other place where flint cobblestones can be found, except on the shores of the English Channel, and as we found many vessels came here from both England and France, it is natural to think that the pile of flint now scattered over a space of about 12 x 20 feet on the flats at the north end of the peninsula, and to be seen only at low tide, was used by the builders of the vessel that carried it as the most convenient and least expensive material to be had where it was constructed, as the custom is here to gather the cobblestones most convenient for ballast.

I have one piece of timber from this locality, and that is marked by having a hole bored through it. No doubt that vessel was built during the good old "Pod-Auger Times" which one of our citizens often sings about. The limestone ballast found further up the river, we trace to the West Indies. Another foreign mineral found on the site of the settlement across the river, is coquina. These mineral relics are the principal and ever lasting remains of former navigation that once made this place famous.

Gone are the ships that brought these fragments to our shore;
Silent are they and yet we wish that they could tell us more,
Still is the voice, and guiding hands
That shaped their course from foreign lands.

CHAPTER XXII.

The Remains of An Old Wharf.

ALTHOUGH there must have been many wharves or landing places for vessels and boats on the shore of these harbors, and up the river at the other settlements, there is only one place I have yet examined that indicates a substantial structure of ancient origin now left.

Beside the destructive work of the worms, as described in the last chapter, there are other agents of perpetual destruction. Unusually high tides, heavy swells, and ice formation on both rocks and timbers, often lift them from their beds, and with the swift current they are carried miles away, landing on some other shore, or in the case of the stone used for ballast on the cob-work wharves, dropped to the bottom of the bay or sea outside, when the sun and warmer water of the ocean loosen the ice grip that picked them up from their former resting place.

A good illustration of this work of destruction by nature has been furnished within the last decade, on the eastern bank of this river, about half way from the mouth to Pemaquid Falls.

A few years ago, 1890, I think, the winter was so mild that very little ice was secured south of New England, and the price ruled high. At Boyd's Pond, a tributary of the Pemaquid, a short distance above the Falls, there was a good supply of excellent quality. A company of Bristol people began operations to cut, stack, ship and market it at New York, where it sold readily at four dollars per ton. Many men with ox and horse teams, were engaged in hauling it from the pond to the shore; a wharf was built, large vessels were filled and dispatched from it. And what remains to be seen of all that industry to-day? Simply *two lone piles* of that wharf, so far upon the bank of the river, that the ice has not yet pulled them from their bed, or with the swift current broken them off, like their companions farther out in the river, where it could reach them.

No stranger that happens to notice those two simple sun-bleached posts, can tell their history; and yet they are a fair example of many simple relics yet found here, all now left to tell the tale of past life and industry connected with them. If in one decade the index of a large industry is nearly obliterated by the natural elements, what can we expect would occur in two or three centuries, with not alone the elements of nature, but the help of man, to obliterate evidence of past occupation.

If "eternal vigilance is the price of liberty," eternal watchfulness is the price of success, in any business connected with the ceaseless changes of the elements about the sea, as every mariner well knows.

A few years ago, a gentleman named William Upham, a former resident of this place, but now of Melrose, Massachusetts, came here with his family on their regular summer vacation tour, to visit their friends and relatives. Having a good opportunity one day, we determined to make an investigation of a spot on the east side of the harbor and river, a little distance above the site of the shipyard and a short distance west of the canning factory. An oval heap of rocks, overgrown with clinging clusters of rockweed, one lone log denuded of the bark, and only partly exposed, were all the visible indications we had to begin with.

With crowbars, shovels and hoe, we soon exposed the framework foundation of the pier of an ancient wharf, about twenty-two feet square, of the type called "cob work," that is, having the logs piled flatways, with the ends across each other, as the country farmers' children pile up corncobs to form their play-houses. The ends of these logs are fitted together by scarfing with an axe, and then secured by great iron bolts driven through them to hold them in place, as is done in building a log cabin. A floor of logs is made over the first layer of the pier, and on that is piled many tons of rocks, which keep the structure from floating, and hold it securely in place.

By clearing away the stone and digging a few hours, we found eleven logs, mostly buried beneath stone and gravel, all lying firmly as originally placed in their beds. The lowest log we excavated, we were surprised to find the bark still sound upon it, and that it was thirty inches in diameter. There are no trees now growing near in this vicinity so large as that. The worm-eaten stumps of upright piling were found buried along the river side of the pier, that were evidently placed there for vessels to lie against while loading or discharging.

We found by measuring, that it was eighty-five feet to the bank of the river. Reason teaches us that that pier must have once been some twelve feet higher than now, as the tide rises from ten to twelve feet here; and there must have been a bridge, with other tiers or strong supports, to connect with the shore. By what other means could the cargoes of vessels landing there have been loaded or discharged? A wharf there would have been in just the right position to connect with the paved street dug up in 1855, by Mr. Varley, which lead down to the shore from the burying-ground.

In close proximity are many old cellars, still to be traced by slight depressions in the soil; one larger than the rest, is said to be the locality of the former Custom House, from which Mr. Alexander Batchelor, who once had charge of the canning factory here, dug out many relics several years ago.

By driving the crowbar deep down in the sand, we traced other timber between the pier and the shore, which must be the foundation of that part connecting it with the mainland. All above the tide water has of course decayed; that below, if there was another pile outside the one examined, must have long since been eaten by the wood worms, but the few remaining timbers of this one being located just between low and high water mark, where they can never become entirely dry to decay, or are continually submerged beneath the water, have escaped destruction thus far. The natural elements have had some assistance on that structure, as well as many others about here, to destroy instead of preserving what remains of interest.

I am informed by Mr. Frank Chadwick, a long time resident of this place, that he can remember when there were many more timbers of this wharf in place on that pier, and a man from New Harbor having a vessel ashore up in McCaffrey's Creek, that he wished to repair, went there, and with a yoke of oxen took away a part of the logs, to shore up or support his vessel while he repaired it. Mr. Partridge found out what he was doing, and stopped him before he got it all torn down. Said he, "Mr. Charles Tibbetts, who died some twenty years ago, at the age of eighty years, told me that that pier stood there when he was a boy, and no one then knew who built it or when it was built."

Mr. Austin Bradley, the modern wharf builder of this locality, said to me, "When we began to build the wharf up there for the canning factory, we intended to have it just where that old one is, but finally built it just above, where it now stands, to get clear of the old one that we found in our way there." I secured two short pieces of the uppermost log; one with a large scarf cut into the side, where the mark of an axe blade could be plainly seen, measuring ten inches across it, indicating that a wide bladed axe did the work. I have secured some relics from each of these places described, to place on exhibition with the other collections here where they belong.

CHAPTER XXIII.

A SHORT distance north of the old fort house, on the south shore of the harbor, there now stands a small building used as a fish-house. Near there a deep square well has been dug to supply water for the canning-factory: a large pile of rough stones that were blown out when the well was dug, still remain close by it. Pointing to the lowest part of that tract of land, which is marked on a map King's Landing, Uncle Jim remarked: "I have ploughed up *showels* and chips of timbers, and suppose that was where the shipyard was located."

I have never been able to find the word "showel" in any dictionary, but ship-builders describe them as pieces of plank laid upon the ground to support the upright parts of their staging and other timbers to hold up the ship's frame while being constructed, which would without them sink deep in the soil, and be unsteady. Uncle Jim had worked several years in shipyards, and consequently ought to be a good judge of the relics which he found there.

When excavations were first made, a barrel or small hogshead was found buried in the ground, the top being covered some two feet below the surface, indicating that the early settlers obtained a supply of water there a long time ago. I secured pipe-fragments, bolts, large hand-made spikes, treenails, and wood with holes bored through it, an odd piece of iron which seemed to have been made for an ornament.

We find a record of several vessels having been built at Pemaquid, in the Massachusetts Archives, Vol. VII., p. 126. "Sloop James and Thomas. Capt. James Bevan, a Quaker affirmed (Quakers are allowed to affirm instead of swearing to a document, as they are allowed to marry themselves, and are exempt by law from going to war, if they do not desire to) — sloop of thirty-five tons burthen, built at Pemaquid in 1695. Capt. John Reed of Antiqua and himself owners. Registered at Boston Nov. 19, 1698." It seems by the foregoing that there were some Quakers or Friends here. There was once a meeting house belonging to that sect at Bremen, and the old burying-ground connected with it is still walled in with stone. They came here soon after the Revolution, and I have never learned of their being persecuted here, or hung for their religious belief, as they were by the Puritans, on the Old Elm of Boston Common. Since the first settlement of this place to the present time, I have never learned of the persecution of any sect or creed for their religious convictions, or of being fined or imprisoned, as the Quakers were by the Pilgrims of the Plymouth Colony from 1660 to 1684.

While visiting at Mr. James Donnell's, a descendent of one of the Friends formerly residing at Bremen, they told me many stories about the early Friends or Quakers, their meeting-house, burying-ground, etc. One of their number who always had been a consistent member of the society, had been greatly annoyed by the depredations of the British during the War of 1812. He came into the house one day in a great rage, and stripping off his swallow-tail coat, and broad-brimmed gray hat, flung them down in one corner of the room, with the exclamation "Thee lay there Quaker till we thrash these British scoundrels." Then he joined his neighbors and assisted to drive the enemy from their shores.

The following are some of the names of the Friends connected with the Bremen meeting: "Ezekiel Farrar, Wm. Keene, Hanna Farrar, John Donnell, James Warner, Wm. Hilton and wife, and Peter Hussey, were prominent members of the society during the latter years of its existence. Peter Hussey was a man of considerable influence in the community, and was a member of the board of selectmen for several years (1820 – 1822)."

As but few people are familiar with the marriage ceremony of the Friends, it may be interesting to learn about it. When a couple desire to join their fortunes by married life, they meet at the public place of worship of the society, and after the usual exercises of the society, they stand facing the audience, and joining hands, make the following vows to each other: "I, Samuel Jones take this my friend Mary Stinson, to be my lawful wife, promising to be to her a faithful and affectionate husband until death shall separate us." The lady then performs her part. "I, Mary Stinson take this my friend Samuel Jones, to be my lawful husband, promising to be to him a faithful and affectionate wife, until death shall separate us." They then register their names on the book of the society, with that of their best man and brides-maid as witnesses, with all the people assembled, and the ceremony is usually closed with a prayer by the minister.

CHAPTER XXIV.

THE OLD BURYING-GROUND.

Smile on, fair river, flowing to the sea,
And chant, O Sea, your anthem evermore,
Seasons shall roll, and human life shall be
Golden with hope as life hath been before;
The sacred records of the dead remain,
And faithful history calls them from the past;
Their feet shall tread with ours the distant plain,
Whose shining space outspreads sublime and vast.

The tumult of the nations rises still,
The shout of war, the grateful hymn of peace;
The torch of science gleams from hill to hill,
While glowing stores in realms of art increase;
And some more prosperous city yet may rise
O'er ancient Jamestown with its field of graves,
And passing ships may hail with glad surprise
Its white towers gleaming o'er the glittering waves.

M. W. HACKELTON.

SIX granite and marble monuments are the most conspicuous objects now visible inside the rough stone wall enclosure of to-day. When Mr. Partridge came here, much of the upper end of the field had become a public burial-ground, and people were brought here from the Point, New Harbor, Long Cove and other places, for burial. He said, "I thought they would bury my field all over, so I had to fence in that place to prevent it."

First a wooden rail and slat fence was erected, supported by iron posts set into large stones. When that decayed about 1875, an organization was formed of people from different parts of the town, who had friends and relatives buried there,

Part of the Ancient Burying Ground in the Fort Field

Gravestone of Morgan McCaffery and others, Date of 1768. The Oldest Found Here is 1695. The Oldest at Plymouth, 1684. People did not Bring Gravestones with them when they came to this Country

place of those long since forgotten, or who perhaps were too poor to obtain them from across the ocean, before they were made here, or they might have shared in the belief of many others of their time, thinking it was wrong to have anything put up to mark their final resting place. When they got so they would sanction a headstone, another period of time elapsed before they would sanction dates and names.

As an illustration, we have a natural stone, about three feet long and about one wide in the widest part, that used to stand in the field, about one-hundred feet northwest of the entrance to the present yard. The inscription upon it reads as follows: "HM. 1695." H. M. are said to be the initials for Sergeant Hugh March. The earliest at Plymouth is 1684.

From Johnson's history we learn that on "September 9th (1695), as a number of men were rowing a gondola 'around a high rocky point above the barbacan,' at the entrance of the harbor, they were fired upon by some Indians, and four killed and six wounded. The killed were Serg. Hugh March, Ed. Sargeant, John Linkhorn, and Thos. Johnson."

In 1888, I found this stone lying against the inside of the western wall of the yard, minus a good sized fragment from the upper corner, that robs it of half the figures of the date, the earliest cut on any stone found here. Fortunately a record of the inscription was secured before it was defaced. I got permission of the owners of the place, to remove the stone to a place of safety, where any one interested can see it.

Another tablet used to stand in the field near the same locality as the one above mentioned. During the winter of 1896, I met Miss Margaret Martin and her brother, then residing on Pemaquid Point; they both had retentive memories and told me many tales of the old settlers. In answer to my question about the old tablet, Miss Martin said, "I remember there used to be a grave there marked with a thick plank at the head, with the name of a lady and other inscriptions on it.

The letters were carved out of the wood, and lead run in to fill the spaces."

Parson Alexander McLain was sent for, to translate the inscription on it, and learned that it was the wife of a French Admiral, that died on board his ship in this locality, and he had her remains brought up there in a boat and buried. They said the name was Abishable or Abashabee Hunt. Capt. Robert Martin, her brother, said, "My father and Jim Curtis went up to the beach clamming, and Jim wanted some lead to run up into shot, to shoot birds with, and he pried out the lead with his jack-knife. He had a "bran" new one, and he broke the blade off. There was a round piece of lead as big as a saucer, nailed on to the headboard, with the likeness of a woman on it."

Mr. Partridge informed me that soon after he came here, a stranger called on him and requested permission to dig open that grave, but he would not give his consent; but the man got up in the night and dug up the remains, and then told Mr. Partridge that he had found them to be those of a woman, as he could tell by the hair and bones. By his mysterious actions, Mr. Partridge thought he had some other object in view beside that of satisfying his curiosity as to the sex of the person buried there.

Soon after I came here, Mr. Samuel Martin, a brother of Margaret and Capt. Robert, rode up to the Jamestown, and as he sat in the wagon, I inquired if he could remember of seeing any graves of people that were buried in the field, between the southern wall and the shore of the creek, pointing to the locality which we could plainly see. "Yes," said he, "I remember when Capt. N. owned this place; he did not care for God, man, or the d—l, and he made his men plough right over them graves, and one of the oxen broke through into one that caved in and they had hard work to get him out again."

Some four years ago, as I stood on the Old Fort Rock with a small company of people, after showing the different points of historic interest in plain view from that location, the antiquity of the old burying-ground was referred to. I remarked that I had never known a grave to be dug there without finding the remains of those previously buried. One of the company, Mr. Robert Poland, then remarked, "Yes, I used to dig graves there forty-eight years ago, and I have taken out the skull and other bones of a dozen people while digging one grave."

After some Indian raid and massacre of the settlement, a large number might have been buried in one grave; on no other occasion would they be likely to be buried in that manner.

Mr. Partridge told me the following story: "Soon after that wall was built, a family from the Point having an interest with the new organization for its care and protection, decided to remove some of the remains of their friends, then buried there, to this yard. It was done while I was gone away to camp-meeting." (It was his custom to take his wife and attend camp-meeting every year, and they would sometimes be away two weeks visiting their friends and relatives in the country.) "When I returned I found they had buried three of *their* people there, and dug up the remains of *four* others and left their bones on the surface of the ground."

From the accounts I have heard of remains of human beings found in and about this yard and the old forts on Fish Point, and other places in this vicinity, it seems Mrs. Hackelton was right, when in her beautiful poem she refers to "Ancient Jamestown with its field of Graves."

Most of the old slate stones remaining in the yard to-day, have queer inscriptions to ornament the face of the headstones, representing weeping willows, skulls, and cross-bones. Some of the headstones bear queer epitaphs. The headstone of Morgan McCaffrey, previously spoken of in the chapter on "old cellars," has the following quaint inscription: "In

Tablet to Commemorate the First Deed executed in America, Conveying a large portion of Pemaquid to John Brown, by the Indian Sagamore Samoset, in 1625

Morgan Mc'Caffery's Gravestone in the old Burying Ground

one time the Colonial Government having an important dispatch to send through the wilderness to Canada, entrusted one copy with each officer, whose names were Nichols and Rogers, offering as a prize to the one who should first succeed in delivering his dispatch at its destination, the command of this fort at Pemaquid. Nichols got the advantage of his companion by employing an expert Indian guide, and consequently gained the prize. This was a severe disappointment to young Rogers, who was entitled by the natural order of promotion, to be the commander of the fort. This circumstance caused ill-feeling between the two families during the remainder of their lives.

There is history enough connected with this old burial-ground to fill a good sized volume, and all the monuments and tablets connected with it ought to be photographed and their inscriptions preserved.

I took photographs of many of the old tablets several years ago, and with the assistance of Miss Carrie Dodge, we copied the inscriptions on them and had them furnished to the New England Historical Society.

CHAPTER XXV.

VISITS OF THE MAINE HISTORICAL SOCIETY IN 1869 AND 1871.

FROM the reports of the Field Days of the Maine Historical Society, published at the time, I obtain the following account of the exercises : —

After an address of welcome by the Hon. E. W. Farley, in which he called attention to the proposed monument to be erected here, he concluded by saying : "Maine has not had justice done to her historic importance."

Mr. Farley was followed by Hon. E. E. Bourne, president of the Society, who said that evidence is rapidly accumulating, that here the first action of civilization in New England commenced — an important fact. He thought the researches now going on in the great libraries of Europe, would soon result in a mass of testimony with which we shall be able in a few years to satisfy everybody that this was so.

He alluded to the controversy with Massachusetts, as to priority of settlement, and read several extracts from undoubted authorities in regard to Pemaquid. One from Thornton (of Massachusetts) he thought worthy to be inscribed on the proposed monument : "This was the initial of New England colonization." Judge Bourne excused himself from speaking at length, as he said he was suffering from a severe cold and deemed it imprudent to continue.

J. H. Hackelton, Esq., of Bristol, was then introduced. He spoke of the incredulity with which many people regard the evidences of the existence of an ancient city with paved streets at Pemaquid, and said he did not propose to quote history, but would produce a few evidences of what Pemaquid has to say for itself. Mr. Hackelton then proceeded to read extracts from several affidavits, showing what the present inhabitants know about the remains.

Mr. Robbins testified that in 1840–41 a paved street (a section of which was unearthed to-day,) extended from the shore to the old cemetery. The former owners removed all traces possible, owing to the value of the tillage land. He described the street as about fifteen feet wide. He had filled many walled cellars. The walls of Fort Wm. Henry were then exposed from three to five feet above the soil.

Henry Varley testified that in 1835 he was employed by Capt. John Nichols, and was engaged with other men more than one week in digging up the pavement of one street, and filled up twelve walled cellars on the west street, near the bank of the river.

Waterman Hatch testified that in 1825 there was a paved street running from the shore to the cemetery, confirming the statement of Mr. Varley, and stated that he saw twenty cellars on the street which was north of Mr. Partridge's house and extended to the river; also saw a large lot of human bones, dug up near the wall of the Fort, and dug into what appeared to be the remains of a pipe factory.

John Stinson was employed by Capt. Nichols in 1835, to fill cellars; counted three hundred; confirmed the statements of Messrs. Varley and Robbins.

Mr. Hackelton stated that this evidence had been taken at different times and places, and most of it sworn to before him as justice. That there were also cellars at Fish Point, where the porgy oil factory is now, unfortunately, situated. [The porgy oil business no longer flourishes here, because the fish do not visit these shores, as formerly. A summer hotel is now kept here, called the Waneta, by Mrs. Roxy Varley.—Ed.] There was also a settlement at Long Cove and New Harbor. John Brown resided at New Harbor, who is referred to in the first deed.

A Mr. Thompson of New Harbor testified that seventeen cellars were found there under a heavy growth of wood, near the shore, and a fort 51x52 feet, with walls five feet thick, on which large oaks were growing forty-seven years ago.

The speaker then gave some statements in regard to a millstone and other relics found in the vicinity, one of which was evidently a leaden tag, such as was formerly used on imported broadcloth, and bore the date of 1610.

The next speaker was Charles H. Tuttle, Esq., of Boston, who commenced by alluding to the wreck of the ship "Angel Gabriel" in Pemaquid Harbor, in 1635. An ancestor of his, John Tuttle, was one of the passengers in this ship, and saved from the wreck the Geneva Bible, which was exhibited to the society at Portsmouth last year. He said he had been surprised to-day at what he had seen. He had heard of paved streets at Pemaquid, as perfect as any in Boston—a fact that many Massachusetts men find it hard to believe—but to-day he had seen and walked upon the pavement and was now convinced. The present Governor of Maine, William T. Haines, is a descendant of Deacon Haines, who was also wrecked at that time.

Charles Dean, Esq., Secretary of the Massachusetts Historical Society, spoke enthusiastically of the magnificent bays and headlands of this coast, and of the beautiful scenery in the vicinity. Alluding to the mysteries of the ancient settlement, he said that one reason we have no account of it is that the chain of tradition was broken by the entire depopulation of the place, and more than twenty years elapsed before it was resettled. Maine, he said, was the oldest spot on the earth, for here were Laurentian hills, and here the green fields first appeared above the waste of waters. Maine, therefore, can claim great antiquity.

Prof. John Johnston, of Middletown, Connecticut, then addressed the meeting and gave many interesting items in relation to the place. Prof. Johnston was then about to publish a history of Pemaquid.

The exercises at the stand here terminated, and the assembly, at about 4 P. M., adjourned to the dinner tent, where a bountiful collation had been prepared.

Owing to the great disappointment of the people at the non-arrival of so many persons by the barge, it was decided to continue the exercises another day, and word was accordingly sent to the surrounding towns to that effect.

THE SECOND DAY.

The weather proved fine on Friday, and at an early hour the people began to assemble. The Damariscotta Cornet Band was on hand and added to the pleasure of the occasion by discoursing fine music.

Long Cove sent a delegation of singing maidens in a gaily decorated rustic car, and heavily loaded boats and teams came from all the country around.

At 11 A. M. the assembly was called to order by the chairman, and the proceedings were opened with prayer by Rev. Wm. A. Drew of Augusta.

Mr. Blaney then made some remarks concerning the monument, and announced that a site for it had been donated by Mr. Partridge, the owner of the land on which they were assembled. He also said that the books were now opened and that one dollar would make any one a member of the Association.

Judge Bourne then resumed his remarks and repeated his quotation from Thornton, that "to Pemaquid we must look for the initiation of civilization into New England," which he deemed of the utmost importance, coming as it did from a Massachusetts man. He also quoted from Increase Mather and others. Mr. Bourne said we don't set up anything against the Pilgrims, and paid an eloquent tribute to those brave men who landed on Plymouth Rock, in the course of which he said that there is no evidence that the Pilgrims ever persecuted any one. He mentioned as a curious fact that in the Massachusetts almanacs, from 1770 to 1820, no mention is made of the landing of the Pilgrims! So he thought nothing could be said about our commencing the observance of our anniversaries at so late a date.

The speaker endeavored to get up a good-natured discussion on some of these historical questions with Mr. Dean of Boston, but in reply Mr. Dean said he was a native of Maine, and as this was not "Popham Day" he didn't propose to enter into any discussion. He then gave some facts in relation to the early voyages, and stated that Pemaquid was first mentioned by name in a paper called "A Description of Mavooshen," in 1602–3–4, up to 1609, which calls the river Pemaquid, although not correct in its location. Strachey's narrative speaks of the "little river Pemaquid." Capt. Smith landed at Monhegan in 1614; mentions a ship of Sir Francis Popham lying at Pemaquid, which he puts down as "St. John's town." The bay is now known as John's bay.

Mr. C. H. Tuttle then made some remarks, in which he said that we had here relics of an archæology not found in Massachusetts. There they had records of all the places from settlement; here we had ruins of a people whose very existence was forgotten. We found here spoons made in the reign of Elizabeth, and pipes dating from 1600.

Mr. Tuttle was interrupted in the very commencement of his remarks by the call to dinner, much to the regret of the audience, who manifested unusual interest in his address, and expected it to be resumed after dinner, but for some reason it was not.

Dinner was served in the big tent, and after the wants of the inner man were attended to, the crowd again assembled at the stand.

President Wood, late of Bowdoin College, was introduced and spoke at some length. In the course of his remarks he mentioned that he had just overheard a young lady remark of the members of the Historical Society present : "If these are fossils they are the spryest fossils I ever saw !" He paid a well merited tribute to the hospitality of the people of Bristol, and expressed his pleasure at finding so much interest in historical matters manifested by them.

The chairman here introduced to the audience Mrs. Foster of Rockport, a descendant of Thos. Gyles of Pemaquid, whose house was burned and himself and a part of his family murdered by the Indians in 1689.

A poem entitled "A Tale of the Winding River," was then read by its author, Mrs. M. W. Hackelton of Bristol. It was a fine production, and was beautifully and impressively delivered by its fair author, who was loudly applauded.

At 2 P. M. the meeting was adjourned to the tent and there continued by remarks from Messrs. Farley, Hackelton, Drew, Blaney, and others, after which the Committee of the Society visited the Lewis farm on the opposite side of the river, and examined the remains of fortifications, cellars, tan-pits, etc., at that place—the remains of a settlement of which there is no history or tradition.

CHAPTER XXVI.

Fortifications.

PROBABLY no other place in the United States has equal distinction with the Old Fort Rock of Pemaquid, in having four forts built and destroyed before the Union of States was formed. Here, too we claim the fierce buzz of the deadly round bomb-shells first startled the English colonists; as fragments of the shells have been gathered about here for many years. None of the battles fought here were very sanguinary or desperate in comparison with those of modern warfare. The caliber of the guns was small; the shot, shell, and fragments of guns found here recently are of rude make. About one mile seems to be the distance the shot could be fired by the French guns. It must be remembered that fighting between ships and stone fortifications may be said to have been in its infancy and both parties in the case of attack on the first stone fort here exhibited their lack of experience in this kind of warfare. The French, awed by the formidable appearance of Fort William Henry, sailed away without firing a shot. Then, when three frigates put in an appearance on one side and hundreds of Indians on the other, and the murderous shells dropped down among them from the high hills beyond the river, the English were terrified by threats of horrid treatment by the Indians, and surrendered, after one day of resistance, a fort which the French commander afterwards acknowledged he doubted if he could haye captured if the English had held out against him.

But for many years these forts served well their purpose as a safe protection from the Indians after they began to quarrel with the white man. They were a haven of refuge for the people for many miles around. Wherever you may travel about this old town of Bristol you can hear stories of scenes enacted about the forts at Pemaquid handed down by tradition by the older people, and by others back in the country for many miles.

The First Fort Called Pemaquid, or Shurt's Fort

Like the settlements here at different periods, the forts have been distinguished by different names each time they were built anew. The first was called Pemaquid or perhaps Shurt's Fort. No doubt this was a simple block-house, and might have been used for a public storehouse too. One authority gives 1624 as the date of its construction, and informs us that it stood until King Philip's War in 1676.

There could have been no necessity for protection from the natives, at least the noble tribe of Wawenocks, for we have shown that they were friendly to the whites. Prof. Johnston writes, " It seems to have been intended rather for a protection against renegades and pirates that were beginning to infest the coast. " " One of those men was Mr. Isaac Allerton, a passenger on the Mayflower, who was discarded by the Pilgrims. He chartered a ship in England, loaded her heavily, and set forth again with a most wicked and drunken crew. He set up a company of base fellows and made them traders to run into every hole and into the river Kennebec in a manner altogether contrary to the established rules of trade. Among the noted characters of that period who sought illegal trade with the natives, was the pirate Dixie Bull. One of the vessels captured by him was commanded by Capt. Anthony Dix, who came to Plymouth in 1623."

Coming to Pemaquid in 1632, he seems not to have met much resistance in his attack on the fort, and soon plundered it and many of the neighboring planters. Bull lost one of his principal men by a shot fired by one of Shurt's men, as he was about weighing anchor in haste to escape the fury of the gathering people now aroused to vengeance.

Information of Bull's plunderings here was transmitted to Gov. Winthrop at Boston, and four small vessels with forty men were sent here and others joined in the pursuit, but the pirates had gone east and escaped. Little more is known of Dixie Bull, but it is said he was finally taken to England, where he suffered the just reward of his villainous deeds.

CHAPTER XXVII

Fort Charles

FORT Charles, which has been described in a previous chapter, page 70, was the second fort erected here. It was built in 1677 under the direction of Sir Edmond Andros when colonial governor of New York, and this territory at that time was called Cornwall. Like the first it was also a wooden fort, two stories high, with a stockade, or high fence, to keep the Indians away from it. At the time this fort was destroyed, August, 1689, the English and French were not engaged in open warfare, but Castine was smarting under the insult of Sir Edmond Andros in the year previous when he pillaged his home at Castine and so was ready to urge and assist the Indians in their work of destruction. Very carefully laid plans were matured for the attack. The destruction of this fort was evidently planned at Castine by Baron De Castine and M. Thury, the Jesuit priest.

From Professor Johnston's History of Bristol, I gather some of the statements in the following narrative of the affair. The number of Indians who engaged in the expedition is supposed to have been over one hundred. To secure the aid of the God of battles, they all confessed and partook of the sacrament; made arrangements with the priest for their wives and children to continue the same devotions during the whole time they should be absent fighting against the heretics, as they called the English,—even during the time usually allowed for sleep,—by establishing a perpetual rosary in their chapel.

Three canoes were sent on ahead, to see that the way was

Sir Edmund Andros

clear, and the plan was for them to wait two leagues from the fort. It seems that Round Pond must have been their place of meeting. After landing they marched in a body with great caution toward the settlement. Charlevoix tells that on their way they took three prisoners from whom they learned that there were about one hundred men in the fort and village, scattered about their work, unconscious of danger."

Mather's account says, "On August 2d, one Starkey going early in the morning from the fort at Pemaquid into New Harbor, fell into the hands of the Indians who, to obtain his own liberty informed them that the fort had at that instant but few men in it, and that one Mr. Giles with fourteen men, was gone up to his farm, and the rest scattered abroad about their occasions. The Indians hereupon divided their little army; part going up to the Falls, killed Mr. Giles and others; part upon the advantage of the tide, took the rest before they could recover the fort."

No attack by the Indians upon a civilized settlement was ever better planned than this, or more completely carried out. The party sent to the fort, when the attack began, took their position between the fort and the village so as to prevent any communication between them, and to cut off the men as they came in from the fields; while the party sent to the falls took care to intercept any that might attempt to escape in the direction of the fort. Besides this, the attack seems to have been made at the time of low water, when the boats in which the men had gone up from the fort could not be made available. All the arrangements had been made with such profound secrecy that the surprise of the English was complete; until the moment the attack began, the English had no suspicion of their presence. The fight began by a furious rush of the Indians upon the fort and village; and the report of their guns seems to have been the signal for the other parties at a distance to perform the parts assigned them. A very few of the inhabitants were so fortunate as to get within the fort;

and, by the terms of capitulation the next day, were allowed to depart with the soldiers to Boston, but nearly all were either killed or taken captive.

According to Charlevoix, immediately after the attack began, the commander of the fort opened fire upon the besiegers with his heavy cannon, but it had no effect to prevent the Indians from taking possession of ten or twelve stone houses, which were situated on a street leading from the village to the fort. They also took shelter behind a large rock, which stood near the fort on the side towards the sea, and in the cellar of a house near by, from both of which places they kept up such a fire of musketry upon the fort, that no one could show his head above the ramparts. This was continued from the time the fight began, about noon, until night; and when it ceased, on account of the darkness they summoned the commander to surrender the fort into their hands, and received as a reply from some one within that " he was greatly fatigued, and must have some sleep."

During the night a close watch was kept to prevent any one from going in or out of the fort, and at day dawn, the firing on both sides was renewed, but in a little time the fire from the fort ceased and the commander proposed to capitulate it. Terms being agreed upon, the commander soon came out, at the head of fourteen men, these being all that remained of the garrison. With them came some women and children, all with packs upon their backs.

The terms of surrender included the men of the garrison, and the few people of the village who had been so fortunate as to get into the fort, with three English captives who had previously escaped from the Indians, but were now in the fort. They were also allowed to take of their effects whatever they could carry in their hands, and to depart in a sloop taken by the Indians the day before, from Capt. Padeshall, who was killed as he was landing from his boat. Two others, Capt. Skinner and Farnham, were, in like manner, shot down as they were stepping on shore from a boat, returning from one of the islands.

In accordance with the terms of capitulation, Weems and his men, with a few others who were with him in the fort, were permitted to depart for Boston ; but all the people of the place, men women and children, who were not in the fort, and had not been killed in the fight, were compelled to leave with the Indians for the Penobscot river, where little was expected but hardship and suffering, scarcely less to be dreaded than death itself. They made the passage, some in birch canoes, and the rest in two captured sloops. The whole number of captives thus taken was about fifty ; but how many were killed we have no means of knowing.

Charlevoix expressly affirms, that after the surrender the Indians allowed those within the fort to depart without being molested, and contented themselves by saying that if they (the English) were wise they would not return again to the place, as the Abenaquis had had too much experience of their perfidy to allow them to remain in peace ; that they were masters of the country, and would never suffer to live there a people so inquiet as they, and who gave them (the Indians) so much trouble in the exercise of their religion. In one of the cellars he says they found a hogshead of brandy ; but they carried their heroic self-denial so far that they destroyed it without even tasting it !

That Weems acted hastily in surrendering the fort as he did, without further effort in self-defense, is very plain ; but we have reason to believe the result would have been no less disastrous if the struggle had been prolonged. How many of his men were killed during the fight, we may not certainly know ; but he had with him at the beginning just thirty, and according to Charlevoix, there were only fourteen left besides himself at the time of the surrender. The number of soldiers killed therefore was sixteen, but the same author says the English allowed only a loss of seven. He, however, intimates that the new-made graves inside the walls showed a greater number of burials. Weems himself was badly burned in the face by an accidental explosion of some gunpowder.

According to Charlevoix, some of the Indians, after thoroughly destroying everything about the fort and settlement at Pemaquid, desired to proceed further, and drive the English from an island three or four leagues distant, but the greater part were opposed to it. The island referred to, very probably was either Monhegan, or one of the Damariscove group, where there may have been a few settlers, or fishermen's huts, of which no record has been preserved.

"A List of ye men that was under ye Command of Lieut. James Wemmes when ye Enemy did attack that Garrison at Pemaquid in August, 1689."

Rodger Sparkes gunr,
Paul Mijikam Surgt,
Jones Marroday Copl,
Robert Smith Drume^{r}
Rutland Clay,
John Pershon,
William Gullington,
Brugan Org,
Richard Dicurows,
Thomas Mapleton,
Richd Clifford,
John Boirnes,
Thomas Barber,
Henry Walton,
Robt Jackson,
William Jones,
Mat Taylor
Fred^{ck} Burnet,
Robt Baxter,
John Bandles,
Thomas Shaffs,
John Allen,
Rodger Heydon,
Joseph Mason,
John Herdin,
Benj. Stanton,
Robt Lawrence,
Thomas Baker,
Orrel James,
Ralph Praston.

"Lieutenant Weems' Accompt of his Pay and Disbursements at the Garrison of Pemaquid, From the 18th day of April, 1689 unto the 13th day of August Ensueing being 117 days.

To the Lieut. pay and his servants a 4 pence pr Diem	£27— 6
To ye Gunners pay a 18 do pr day	8—15—6
To ye Sergeants pay a 18 do pr Diem	8—15—6
To ye Corporals pay a 12 do pr day	5—17
To ye Drums pay a 12 do pr day	5—17
To the pay of 30 Private men at 6 do pr Diem	87—15
To Cash Paid for fyre and Candles	7— 0
To Boat hyre in Several Times to give Intelligence to Boston of ye Condition of the Garrison	6— 0
	£157— 6

JAMES WEEMS."

The following "Relation of Grace Higiman," which was copied from the Mass. Archives, 8 V., 36 Page, may be of interest to the reader :—

"Grace Higiman saith That on the second day of August, 1689, the day when Pemaquid was assaulted and taken by ye Indians, I was there taken Prisoner and carried away by them, one Eken, a Canadian Indian, pretending to have a right in me, and to be my master. I apprehend that there were between two and three hundred Indians at that assault (and no French) who continued there for two days, and then carried away myselfe and other Captives (about fifty in number) unto the Fort at Penobscot. I continued there about three years, removing from place to place as the Indians occasionally went, and was very hardly treated by them, both in respects of Provisions and clothing, having nothing but a torn blanket to cover me during the winter seasons, and oftentimes cruelly beaten. After I had been with the Indians three years, they carried me to Quebeck, and sold me for forty crowns unto the French there, who treated me well, gave me my liberty, and I had the King's allowance of Provisions, as also a Room provided for me, and liberty to work for myselfe. I continued there two years and a halfe, During which time of my abode there, several of the Eastern Indians came, viz., Bomaseen, Moxis his son, and Madockawando's son and divers others, and brought in English Prisoners and Scalps, and received as the French told me, for each scalp (being paid by the Intendent) Twenty French Crowns, according to a Declaration which the Governor there had emitted for their encouragement, and the Captives they sold for as much as they could agree with the purchasers. The Indians also had a Reward offered them for bringing Intelligence from time to time. Soon after the Submission made by the Indians at Pemaquid in 1693, Bomaseen came to Quebeck and brought a paper containing the Substance of the articles of submission, which he showed unto me, and told me that the Governour of Canada said to him, That he should not have made Peace with the English and that he seemed to be much displeased for their having done so, however said they might carry it friendly to the English, till they should meet with a convenient opportunity to do mischief."

French officials in Canada, in the year 1692, claimed that in the various Indian fights of the preceding years, they had destroyed for the New Englanders besides Pemaquid, no less than sixteen pallisaded forts and settlements, in which were twenty cannon and about two hundred men.

Thomas Gyles, above referred to, was one of three brothers who emigrated to this country from Kent, England, probably in 1668 ; the names of the others being James and John. Thomas was one of the chief men of the place, and appears to have carried on a considerable business. On the morning of that memorable day when the fort was captured, with his three eldest sons, Thomas, James and John, and several hired men, he went up to the falls, to work in a field he had there, some at haying, and some at gathering grain. They labored until noon, and took their dinner together at the farmhouse, without suspicion of danger. Having finished their dinner, the men went to their work ; but Mr. Gyles and two of his sons, remained at the house, when suddenly firing was heard from the direction of the fort. Mr. Gyles was disposed to interpret the occurence favorably, and so remarked to his sons ; but their conversation was cut short by a volley of bullets from a party of Indians who had been hitherto concealed, awaiting the signal from the fort to begin their bloody work ! The party of Indians numbered some thirty or forty, who now rising from their ambush, finished their work in a few minutes, killing or capturing all except Thomas Gyles, the oldest son, then about nineteen. Where the latter was when the attack began, we do not know, but he was so fortunate as to make his escape unhurt from the field, and passing down on the west side to Pemaquid harbor, was taken on board a fishing schooner which was just ready to sail.

Thomas Gyles, the father, was mortally wounded by the first volley from the Indians, and afterwards despatched with a hatchet. His son John who was taken captive, says that when the attack was made, "My brother ran one way and I another, and looking over my shoulder, I saw a stout fellow, painted, pursuing me with a gun, and a cutlass glittering in his hand, which I expected every moment in my brains." Falling down the Indians did him no injury, but tied his arms and bade him follow in the direction where the men had been at work about the hay. "As we went," he says, "we crossed where my father was, who looked yery pale and bloody, and walked very slowly. When we came to the place, I saw two men shot down on the flats, and one or two knocked on the head with hatchets. Then the Indians brought two captives, one a man, and my brother James, who with me, had endeavored to escape by running from the house, when we were first attacked."

At length the savages were ready to start with their captives, and the narrative continues, "We marched about a quarter of a mile, and then made halt. Here they brought my father to us. They made proposals to him by old Moxus, who told him that those were strange Indians who shot him, and that he was sorry for it. My father replied that he was a dying man and wanted no favor of them, but to pray with his children. This being granted him, he recommended us to the protection and blessing of God Almighty; then gave us the best advice, and took his leave for this life, hoping in God that we should meet in a better land. He parted with a cheerful voice, but looked very pale, by reason of his great loss of blood, which now gushed out of his shoes. The Indians led him aside. I heard the blows of the hatchet, but neither shriek nor groan. I afterwards heard that he had five or seven shot holes through his waistcoat or jacket, and that he was covered with some boughs."

Thomas Gyles, whose useful and honorable life was thus brought to a close, was a remarkable man. At what time he came to this country is not a certainty, but May 8th, 1669, he purchased land on the north side of the Pejepscot, or Androscoggin river, a few miles below Topsham village, where he located his family and resided several years. His father, who was a man of considerable wealth in England, having died, he, with his family, left for England, probably in 1674, and returned soon after the first destruction of the English settlements in this region. To avoid trouble with the Indians, he removed his family to Long Island, New York, and lived there several years; but fancying that the atmosphere there was not suited to his constitution, and learning that the agents of the Duke of York were about establishing a regular government here, and erecting a fort, he returned to this place, and became a permanent resident. He derived an annual income from the estate of his father in England, and probably was the most wealthy citizen of the place; and being strictly methodical in his habits, he took care to purchase of the constituted authorities, what landed estate he needed, probably about the falls. He also purchased one or more lots near the fort, where the family lived.

He was a man of the most unbending integrity, and always exerted great influence in the community where he lived, but was not particularly popular. In his religious opinions he sympathized with the Puritans, and was very particular in regard to the proper observance of the Sabbath ; and his earnest attempts to discharge every duty as an upright magistrate, sometimes brought him in collision with his neighbors.

Of the two sons, James and John, the former after being in captivity three years, and suffering great hardship, made his escape to New Harbor, with another boy who had been captured at Casco. Here unfortunately, they were both taken prisoners again by the Indians, and returned to the Penobscot, where they were tortured to death at the stake by a slow fire.

John, the other son, after being with the Indians about six years, was sold to a French gentleman, who lived somewhere on the Penobscot. By this man and his family he was treated with much kindness, being known among them as "Little English." Finally, in the summer of 1698, a favorable opportunity occuring for him to secure a passage by a trader to Boston, his master voluntarily gave him his liberty, and he rejoined his two brothers and sisters in Boston, his mother having died several years previously.

As he was about eleven years old when captured at the falls, he was of course now about twenty, with only the little education he had received before his capture. Having obtained a good knowledge of the Indian language, and also the Canadian French, he was often employed by the government, as well as the traders, to act as interpreter with the Indians. In 1700 he received a commission as Lieutenant, and was put under regular pay by the government ; and six years later he was made Captain. In 1725 he superintended the erection of the fort at Brunswick, which was named Fort George. Here he remained ten years, being in 1725 transferred to the command of the garrison on St. George's river. Subsequently, in 1728 he was appointed a justice of peace, which in those days was considered a high honor.

Mr. Gyles in 1736 published a very interesting account of the capture of Fort Charles, and the attending circumstances, and a narrative of events during his residence with the savages. About the same time the garrison at the fort was considerably reduced, and Mr. Gyles retired from the service. The rest of his life was passed in Salisbury and Roxbury. He died in the latter place in 1755, at the age of seventy-seven.

The complete destruction of the fort and settlement at Pemaquid was considered a great achievement by the Indians; and they assured M. Thury, on their return, that with two hundred Frenchmen, a little acquainted with the country, and ready to follow their lead, they would not hesitate to march upon Boston. The same feeling was shown by the French in Nova Scotia and Canada; and from this time hopes began to be entertained by them that they might be able utterly to exclude the English from the continent, at least as far south as New York and New Jersey.

Sir William Phips. native of Maine, first American chosen Governor, and first to be Knighted by the King of England. Builder of Fort Wm. Henry at Pemaquid.

CHAPTER XXVIII.

Fort William Henry 1692–1696.

THE third fort erected here by the energy and influence of Sir William Phips, has an interesting record.

It puzzled me for several years after coming here, to understand why a fort so formidable and expensive was required, as was this first one, built of stone, "away down east." This fortification was designed to declare and to maintain the claim and the rights of the English to the eastern territory, and also to restrain the Indians from encroachment on the western settlements.

The territory called Acadia, whose western boundary was never determined, was passed back and forth between England and France by successive treaties. It had been last yielded to France by the treaty of Breda in 1667, and the surrender of Fort Charles and its destruction, put the French into full possession. But the capture of Port Royal by Phips and his forces in 1680, brought back the eastern country into the hands of the English. To hold it securely was a reason for the rebuilding of the fort at Pemaquid.

A noted Frenchman, Baron De Castine, had secured the good graces of Madockawando, the chieftain of the Penobscot tribe, and had married his daughter. The Indians seem to have been easy converts to the Jesuit's faith and were ready allies with the French against the English colonists. Long and bloody were the struggles on this border land of New England, where the native red man strove to hold "his own, his native land" and the white man struggled for supremacy and possession, till at last the English conquered both the

French and natives, and made vain the former's boast that they would drive them from America, although they once held possession of more territory of this country than the English did.

Sir William Phips, our hero and builder of this fort, and his contemporary, friend and historian, Cotton Mather, like many others connected with the early history of New England, deserve more than a passing notice.

Many noted men of those times were harshly treated by their fellow citizens during their lifetime, because as officers of the home government at England, they were sworn to obey and enforce the laws of their rulers, which so often conflicted with the interests of the colonists here. Impartial writers have recently given us interesting accounts of some of these men : Mather, Phips, Andros, and others.

Sir William Phips was the son of James Phips of Bristol, England, and is said to have been one of a family of twenty-six children. A few quotations from a biographical sketch of Sir Wm. Phips written by Mr. Wm. Goold, are worthy of note here. Referring to Mather, he says, Drake in his life of him says : "Literature owes a vast deal to Cotton Mather, especially for his historical and biographical works. Were these alone to be stsuck out of existence, it would make a void in these departments of literature that would confound many who affect to look upon them with contempt."

The following account will show the connection of Phips with Salem witchcraft, and something of his character :— "When Sir William Phips had well canvassed a cause, which perhaps might have puzzled the wisest men on earth to have managed without an error, he thought if it would be any error at all, it certainly would be safest for him to put a stop unto all future prosecutions, as far as it lay in him to do it.

"He did so, and for so doing had the printed acknowledgments of the New Englanders, who publicly thanked him. The Queen sent him autograph letters commending his

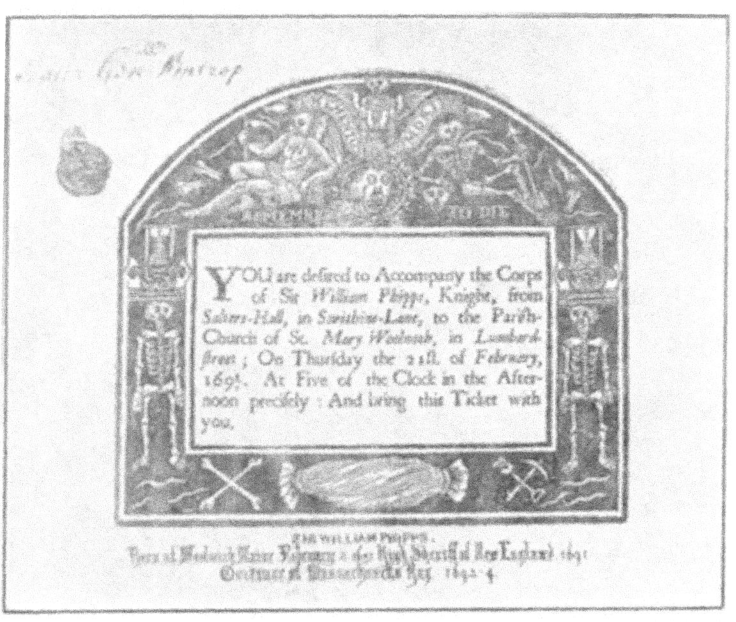

YOU are desired to Accompany the Corps of *Sir William Phipps, Knight*, from *Salters-Hall*, in *Swithins-Lane*, to the Parish-Church of St. *Mary Woolnoth*, in *Lombard-street*; On Thursday the 21st. of *February*, 169$\frac{4}{5}$. At Five of the Clock in the Afternoon precisely: And bring this Ticket with you.

The King's Invitation to the Funeral of Sir William Phips

course. A court of oyer and terminer had been selected from the Councillors to try the witches. Our journalist, Sewall, was a member. They had held two or three sessions before the arrival of the charter, and condemned many. The question coming up in the Council about its sitting again, Sewall represents Governor Phips as saying, "It must fall," and that was the last of it. Governor Phips finally pardoned all those in the prisons accused of witchcraft."

"After the witchcraft mania had begun to subside, Governor Phips turned his attention to the next greatest trouble under which he found the people suffering. That was the French and Indian war. We must again consult his biographer, Dr. Mather, who says: 'Now he was come to the government, his mind was very vehemently set upon recovering of those parts from the miseries which a new and long war of the Indians had brought upon them. His birth and youth in the east had rendered him well known to the Indians there; he had hunted and fished many a weary day in his childhood with them; and when those rude salvages had got the story by the end that he had found a ship full of money, and was now become all-one-a-king! they were mightily astonished at it; but when they further understood that he was become the Governor of New England, it added a further degree of consternation to their astonishment. He was likewise better acquainted with the situation of those regions than most other men.' "

On the arrival of Governor Phips at Boston, May 14, 1692, (from his visit to England) with the new charter and his commission as Governor, he "proceeded to erect a strong fort at Pemaquid such as had never before been seen in all the region." A bill was passed by the legislative assembly, authorizing a tax of £30,000 for general purposes. Nearly £20,000 of that amount was used in paying for the construction of that fort. Having engaged some four hundred and fifty men, and such tools and materials as were needed, he sailed from Boston in August, having with him, Col. Benj. Church, commander of the province forces. On their way they stopped at Falmouth (now Portland) and took on board the large guns which had lain there since the destruction of Fort Loyal, more than two years, and decently buried the bones of the slain which lay bleaching upon the ground.

After coming safely to anchor at Pemaquid Harbor, a site for the new fort was selected, covering the same locality as Fort Charles, but extending a little farther west, so to include the great rock which the Indians had used as a defence when they captured the fort, three years previous. Mather gives the following description of the fort which they constructed in the second volume of his "Magnalia," page 540

Description of Fort William Henry.

"Captain Wing, assisted with Captain Bancroft, went through the former part of the work; and the latter part of it was finished by Captain March. His Excellency, attended in this matter, with these worthy Captains, did in a few months despatch a service for the king, with a prudence, and industry, and thriftiness, greater than any reward they ever had for it. The fort, called the William Henry, was built of stone, in a quadrangular figure, being about seven hundred and thirty-seven foot in compass, without the outer walls, and one hundred and eight foot square, within the inner ones; twenty-eight ports it had, and fourteen (if not eighteen) guns mounted, whereof six were eighteen pounders. The wall on the south line, fronting to the sea, was twenty-two foot high, and more than six foot thick at the ports, which were eight foot from the ground. The greater flanker or round tower, at the western end of this line, was twenty-nine foot high. The wall on the east line was twelve foot high, on the north it was ten, on the west it was eighteen. It was computed that in the whole there were laid above two hundred cartloads of stone. It stood about a score of rods from high water mark;

and it had generally, at least sixty men posted in it for its defence, which if they were men, might easily have maintained it against more than twice six hundred assailants."

The Destruction of Fort William Henry in 1696.

Early in the season, plans for the reduction of New England were discussed by the French officers at Canada and Acadia. The Indians began depredations in New Hampshire and Western Maine. Peace about Pemaquid was due to the presence of the "strongest fastness of the British in North America." This fort was a great annoyance to the Indians because it was directly on their line of travel along the sea coast They would not venture to go around Pemaquid Point in their bark canoes, but would carry them on their heads across the land from New Harbor to Pemaquid Outer Harbor. It was of the utmost importance to both the French and Indians that they should gain possession of this fort.

The Indian trail between these two villages has been pointed out to me at the highest point of land between them, by Mr. Alexander Brackett, who found a fine Indian gouge close by it, when he dug the cellar for his store. (We have it in our collection.) He told me that he owed his life to an Indian doctor of the Penobscot tribe, who with many others used to follow up the custom of their forefathers, by crossing over the same trail yearly. They passed the whole summer on a trip from Old Town, near Bangor, Maine, (where about five hundred still reside) to the head waters of the Sheepscot and return. They were Catholics, and I am told visited a church at Whitefield to have their sins pardoned. Besides the Doctors, Mitchell and Big Thunder, there were others that made baskets, bows, arrows, etc., and sold them to the different villages along their route.

I remember of attending a traveling show given by a company of that tribe at New Harbor, in which their war-dances, their marriage ceremonies, hideous war-whoops, and scalping scenes were most vividly portrayed. A son of Dr. Mitchell visited this place last year, having baskets and small trinkets to sell. I took him across the bay one morning in my little boat to meet the steamer, and he told me several stories of Big Thunder and his father. His family made the goods which he was selling. He expressed regret that he had not followed the profession of his father, (who was familar with 150 different kinds of medical plants) who, he said, became so skillful a physician that he would sometimes be called long distances to attend difficult cases, and would receive as high as eighty and one hundred dollars for a single visit.

The French had two frigates well armed and equipped, on this shore, named l'Envieux and la Profonde, under the command of D'Iberville. They encountered two English ships, the Newport and Sorlings, with a small vessel for a tender, that had been sent east to capture French prizes, but the latter proved too strong for them and captured the Newport, while the other escaped by sailing out of sight into the fog, which fortunately settled down over them just in time. After repairing the ships they sailed for Castine, having taken on board about one hundred Indians as an extra crew; then they found Castine had engaged the services of two hundred of the Penobscot tribe.

Another French officer, Villieu, with twenty-five French soldiers, joined the expedition there, and the three ships sailed together for Pemaquid. The two hundred Indian warriors under Castine, started in their canoes, and reached their destination August 13th, and the three ships under D'Iberville the next day. It is believed they took their position on the western part of John's Bay, having Beaver and John's Islands as a partial means of defense.

At five o'clock P. M. of the 14th, a summons was sent to the fort to surrender. Pasco Chubb, the commander, sent back word that he would not surrender even "if the sea was covered with French vessels, and the land with Indians."

Phips's Point, Woolwich, Maine, Birthplace of Governor Phips

Sieur D'Iberville, the French Officer who Captured Fort Wm. Henry in 1696.

The fighting then began, but little was accomplished on either side that evening. During the night the French landed heavy cannon and mortars, according to the best authority, at the first a little west of the Barbacan, and by three o'clock the next day had them in position on the high bluff near where the Hotel Edgemere was formerly located. No doubt the place was then well covered with trees, which would conceal their movements from watchmen on the fort.

These positions of the ships and battery I think are verified by the position of the cannon balls found here. I have the evidence of Mr. Calvin C. Robbins and William Erskine that a large number of cannon balls were found near the burying-ground year after year, as they were ploughed out of the ground. They were carried to the old barn and barrels of them were finally sold for old junk at one-half cent a pound.

Mr. Allen Lewis and Lyman Curtis, the latter still living, have both told me that when boys they were on board of vessels called "old junkmen" that used to cruise along the shore and sell tinware and calico, as tin peddler with carts, did the same goods by land, taking in exchange old rags, iron, rubber, etc. Other shot of the same caliber have been found south of the village in the garden of Mr. Frank Chadwick. From these two positions named where the shot were found (and some have been found recently) we find the fort to be in range of the positions said to have been occupied by the ships and batteries, and learn the distance they were fired. Evidently, all these shot were intended for the fort, but the French gunners were either poor marksmen, like the Spanish in our late unpleasantness with them ; or they were a long time in getting their true range and wasted much ammunition without avail.

The French, after getting their mortars in place, began throwing bomb-shells at the fort. Doubtless some of them landed inside the walls. We have no means of knowing how many people were gathered there for protection, driven from their homes by fear of the Indians.

I imagine that they and the soldiers then got the greatest surprise of their lives. Here, then, was a new element of destruction, brought into use I think, for the first time in the history of warfare in this country. It is certain the English had no bomb-proof covers for protection for the inmates, only small ones for the powder magazines under the Rock and Bastion. Consternation and despair came with this new shrieking element of destruction, and it seemed that this place of fancied security for themselves and little ones, had now become a slaughter-pen, where they were gathered like a helpless flock of sheep, to perish *en masse*.

Just then Castine offered them another chance to save their lives, by sending a letter into the fort, which informed them if they surrendered they should be transported to a place of safety, and receive protection from the savages; but if they were taken by assault they would have to deal with the Indians and must expect no quarter, for such were the instructions from the king. The History of Bristol and Bremen states, that when Hutchinson wrote his history of Massachusetts he had the original note of Castine before him. When hostilities ceased, the terms of surrender were agreed upon by the officers of the fort, all marched out and were convoyed to one of the adjacent islands for protection from the Indians, and Villieu with sixty French soldiers, took possession. They found an Indian confined with irons in the fort, who had been there a prisoner since a fight between the men at the fort and Indians, on the previous February. He was in a miserable condition, having suffered much from his long confinement.

On learning of his condition, the other Indians were greatly enraged, and it was fortunate that the English had been taken to a place of safety, or they might not have escaped the fury of the savages. Among Chubb's private papers was found an order, recently from the Massachusetts authorities, to hang the wretched Indian prisoner; but the French wisely kept the information from the natives.

The conduct of Chubb in thus surrendering the fort so readily, was severely condemned by the Massachusetts Colony. It was in good condition, had a good bomb-proof magazine, partly under the "Great Rock," fifteen mounted cannon, a garrison of ninety-two men, and sufficient supplies for a long siege. Chubb and his men had only one excuse for so easily giving up the fort, and that was to save the indiscriminate slaughter of innocent and defenseless people, confined within its walls, by the deadly bomb-shell, which they could not resist or offset with like missiles.

The cannon and other property of the fort were then removed on board the French ships, except the small arms, which with much ammunition was distributed among the Indians, much to their satisfaction. The fort and everything about it were destroyed, the walls thrown down as far as possible, and on the eighteenth of the month, they took their departure for the Penobscot.

Chubb was arrested on his return to Boston, and thrown into prison. After several months' confinement he was released, and returned to his family at Andover, Massachusetts, where he and his wife were killed by the Indians, February 22, 1698. About thirty of them visited the place on purpose to avenge the wrongs they believed he had done them.

The following documents from French sources, make an instructive supplement to the story of the taking of Fort William Henry, and are of much importance for comparison with the English documents.

First Document.

From French Documents Found in Manuscript in the Boston Library, and Translated by Rev. Henry O. Thayer.

PLAN FOR THE ENTERPRISE AGAINST PEMAQUID.

If his Majesty would make entirely sure the possession of Acadia, the alliance and fidelity of the savages, and would hinder the English from forming and easily executing their plans for overrunning that section west of the outer St. Lawrence as far as Quebec, it is thought that in the present condition of affairs, that end cannot be attained except by ruining the fort at P. . . . . . situated between the rivers Pentagoet (Penobscot) and Kennebec. There the greater part, and the most warlike of the savages of Acadia, make their home and have established themselves in a kind of villages.

This fort which the English have undertaken to build on the land of France, because it is the river Kennebec which should make the boundary, and which separates it from New England, is situated in a bay over against an island which closes the entrance, and which has on the two sides a channel for the largest vessels. This fort is about 25 fathoms square. The face or curtain, which looks to the south and commands the roadstead, is a wall of 8 or 9 feet in thickness, not terraced more than at the curtains of the fort. Upon this wall are twelve pieces of cannon with their embrasures, and at the end of it and at the angle which looks to the southwest, is a great tower of about five yards in diameter, which is arched. Upon this are five more pieces of cannon, which bear upon the sea. Inside of the arch is the powder magazine.

The three other curtains are walls 4 or 5 feet in thickness, and at the angle which looks to the northeast, there is a little bastion, on which there are three pieces of cannon which bear upon the land. The other two angles are not fortified, although approach to them is easy, and they are not defended only by that tower and that bastion. The lodgings are in sheds along the three curtains that look toward the land. There are loopholes in these walls for the Musketeers.

Out from this bay there is a little harbor, in which the

anchorage at a half league in distance, is good for the largest vessels. From this little harbor, where there are twelve or fifteen houses scattered and dilapidated, to the Fort of P. . . . . it is only three-quarters of league, and there is a cart road fine and new. Sieur de Villebon, who has reconnoitered the whole, disguised as a savage, has recently sent on all the plans of it, and Sieur de Bonaventure has brought away with him from Acadia two men who have been there several times, and who are ready to return with him. Sieur Paquire, the king's engineer, who was conducted there by Sieur de Villebon in 1698, has taken the plan of it, which he sent this time to the court.

Second Document.

For this expedition, it is believed two vessels of war will be necessary, which certainly can be added without any great increase of expense along with what has been sent, which his Majesty pleases to grant annually for Quebec and Acadia, for the subsistence of the troops which he maintains there. . . The two vessels will go to anchor at Mount Desert, which is an isle at the entrance to the river of Pentagoet, where the anchorage is very good and sure, and which is only 15 leagues from Fort P. . . . The commander will find all the savages assembled at Pentagoet according to orders which they received some months previously.

The commander will send a shallop into the river Pentagoet to inform the savages, and then will select the officers to command them and to march with them at a designated day, to a half league of the fort P. . . There they will abide without showing themselves in the wood, taking such position that no one whatever can go out of the fort without falling into their hands. The commander will have distributed to them all food for six days.

Then the vessels will set sail to go to an anchorage in New Harbor, which is the place that has been designated as distant only three-quarters of a league from the fort of P . . . . At this place they will put ashore the commander, the officers, the engineers, the soldiers, cannoniers, bombardiers, and the light artillery and the munitions, as well as those for war as for personal use. While his officers and soldiers shall march to invest the fort in conjunction with the savages, who will join them on the way and will lead on the artillery to attack this fort, the vessels will sail and come round to anchor in the bay under cover of an island which is only a good quarter of a league from the fort, and from whence they can conveniently furnish food and ammunition needed by the officers, soldiers and savages, and at the same time prevent the English frigates from being able to throw reinforcements into this fort.

After the capture and demolition of this fort and its artillery and the embarkation of officers and soldiers, they will distribute to the savages all the remaining provisions which had been provided for them for this expedition. Then having incited them to make incursion into the enemy's country, the vessels will weigh anchor to go to their destination.

Third Document

Whoever it may be who has said that the taking of the fort of Pemkuit would protect the French fisheries on the shores of Acadia and the river of Quebec, and would prevent those parties which can come to Montreal and Quebec from the borders of the English and the Iroquois,—such a one is foolish and does not know the country; but what one can say with reason is this:—that the taking of the fort of Pemkuit which very greatly inconveniences the Canebas and Abenakis, will assure their friendship; and if these savages had united with the English it would not have been safe to make a settlement in the section south of the river of Quebec, and also that those savages form a barrier for Canada, which comprises La Cadie (Acadia) and extends as far as opposite to Quebec. This is what is true and what will always be reasonable to say.

FOURTH DOCUMENT

LETTER OF THE MINISTER TO MONS. BEGON.

VERSAILLES 22 Febr 1696.

I have written in your absence to Mons Manclerc that the king has assigned the [war-]ship the "Envious," and the store-ship the "Profound" armed for war, for the voyage to Acadia. His Majesty has resolved to make an attack on the fort which the English have at the entrance to the river of Pemaquid.

There are needed for this purpose some provisions of which you will find a list appended to this, for subsistence of the savages which will be employed on this expedition.

It is needful for you to have them provided. On your advising me what they will cost I will have the funds remitted to you for them.

Statement of provisions for the reinforcement and for a particular service, which will be shipped on the vessels the "Envious" and the "Profound."

40 barrels of meal at 4 l 10c per quintal	1400
10 quarters of bacon at 33 l	330
300 lb do of lard at 8c the p	120
60 bushels of peas at 55c	165
2 barrels of eau de vie [brandy] at 70 l	140
300 lb of Brazillian tobacco at 15c	225
one barrel of Bordeaux prunes	28
Total amount for provisions	2408 li

ARTILLERY, ARMS, MUNITIONS

2 Brass cannon for 12lb ball, with their field carriages and necessary implements.

2 Brass mortars of 11 to 1200lb with their carriages and implements for the same M. d'Iberville has brought back two of them from his expedition.

400 balls, 200 bombs and the necessary powder for the cannon and mortars.

600lb of gunpowder.

1000lb of lead in balls.

3000 gun flints.

300 worm-screws [or gun-worms.]

50 powder horns.

50 service sabres } these two articles will be brought back to
20 service guns } the armory from which they shall be taken.

200 light grenades.

Two campaigning wheels [wheels for the land] six feet in diameter.

Four pieces of iron [or masses of unwrought iron] weighing 8, 10, 12, and 15 lbs.

30 pick-axes.

12 picks.

10 spades.

20 shovels, iron bound [or tipped.]

40 medium Swiss axes.

6 augers.

3000 assorted nails.

All which can not be of service, or shall not be fully used, will be returned to the armory from which they shall be taken.

Fifth Document.

Instructions to Sieur D'Iberville Commander of the King's Ships — "L'Envieux" and the "Profound."

Versailles, 28 Mars, 1696.

"If [certain vessels are not on the coast etc.] His Majesty thinks it the most advantageous course that he should go with the "Envieux" which he commands and the "Profound" commanded by Sieur de Bonaventure, directly to Pentagoet to undertake the execution of the enterprise against Pemaquid before their arrival on the coast is known in Boston."

[If at Pemaquid he does not find the savages assembled nor soon to be, then go to St. John's river first.]

"After the taking of the fort of Pemaquid and putting himself into a state to make defence in case he should be attacked there during the little time he will have to stay on land, he should go to work without any delay, to demolish and entirely to destroy the fortifications and generally all the vessels of Pemaquid and the vicinity if any are there, employing for the purpose all his men that he can, and especially the savages, in order that this destruction may extend to the foundations, by the work of the hand, and by fire and mines, and he will prepare a report and have it certified by the officers present."

Sixth Document.

Report from M. de Champigny.

Quebec, 25th October, 1696.

Count Frontenac received at Quebec letters from M. Thury, Missionary in Acadia, of 25 of May, by which he learned what had occurred at Pemaquid fort, between the Abenaquis savages and the English.

There had been a project for an exchange of prisoners of which Sieur St. Castine took charge in behalf of M. Count Frontenac. No more interested or intelligent an agent could be chosen.

Some Frenchmen had been employed to carry letters to the governor of Boston, by which to determine the place for the negotiations. But as they could not accomplish it, they were obliged to engage some savages, who carried the letter which the English prisoners wrote to the officers who commanded Pemaquid fort.

The officer knew so well how to turn the minds of those savages, that he persuaded them to come to his fort, to obtain what would be necessary for them, promising that the trade should be carried on in good faith. Taxus, an important chief of Abenaquis, first fell into the snare, and in spite of the remonstrances of M. Thury, who showed the difficulties into which their credulity would bring them, and who separated from them and withdrew into the woods, with as many as he could draw — was followed by many others who all went to the English fort.

They traded there peacefully several days, but at length the prophecies of their Missionaries proved true ; the English, seeing these principal chiefs assembled within range of the musketry of the fort, commenced by killing Edzerimet [Egeremet ?] a famous chief and his son, by pistol shots. Taxus was seized by three soldiers and some others likewise, one of which was carried off alive into the fort ; two others got free by using their knives upon the three enemies who had each seized them, and it cost the lives of four English. One of our savages lost his life by shots fired from the fort ; another saved Taxus, who had also killed two enemies with his knife. So this treachery has caused us to lose four men and our enemies six.

Some Abenaquis and other savages of Kennebec surprised on some islands opposite the fort, a detachment from the garrison of Pemaquid and killed twenty-three of them.

. . . .

The two ships of the King, the "Envious" and the "Profound" with their prize Newport, returned at length to Pentagoet where, after trading with the savages and distributing the King's presents, they embarked two hundred and forty of them ; at the head of which was Sieur St. Castine and twenty-five soldiers detached from the company of Sieur Villieu with their captain and S. Montigny, his lieutenant.

They anchored before Pemaquid on the 10th of August. S. d'Iberville at once summoned the fort to surrender, which the commander refused to do. Then he landed two field guns and two mortars. The batteries were placed in a little time and they were satisfied with firing four bombs which they threw over beyond the fort.

Again the summons was made with a declaration to give them no quarter, if they did not heed it. They accepted the orders of S. d'Iberville to go out with their clothing only, on condition of being sent to Boston and exchanged for French or savages who should come in there as prisoners. S. d'Iberville took possession of the fort : an Abenaquis captured at the same time as Edzrimet had been killed. As we have said, the garrison consisted of ninety-two men, without reckoning any women and children.

There were in this fort fifteen pieces of cannon : the guns and other munitions of war were given up to the savages to recompense them for the losses which the fort had caused them.

SEVENTH DOCUMENT.

[FROM PARIS DOCUMENTS, IN COL. HISTORY OF N. Y.]

Accounts of provisions and stores for an attack on the fort.

Two months' provisions to be brought for the subsistance of the Indians estimated at 200 men to be loaded equally in the 3 vessels.

2000 lbs. of flour.
2 tierces molasses to flavor their sagamite.
200 lbs. of butter for the same purpose.
10 bbls. of brandy ; without which it will be impossible to prevail on them to act efficiently.

In order to avoid incumbering the ships, the surplus of provisions they may require during two months, can be sent for, on their arrival to Minas or Port Royal, where they could be procured cheaper than in France, and be advanced by the Company's Agent who is in that Country.

Memorandum of presents for the Indians of Acadia, for the sum 3640li which his Majesty grants them in order to wage war against the English.

2000 lbs Powder.
40 bbls. of Bullets.
10 " " Swan shot.
400 lbs. of Brazilian Tobacco.

200 Tomahawks of which M. de Bonaventure will furnish the pattern.

60 selected guns like those of this year.

200 Mulaix shirts averaging 30s each.

8 lbs. of fine vermillion.

200 tufts of white feathers to be given the Indians in order to designate them during the night in case of attack, and which will cost at most only six at 7c ; to be selected in Paris by M. de Bonaventure.

Which presents will be distributed among the Indians when they will be all assembled at the rendezvous to be indicated to them.

CHAPTER XXIX.

Fort Frederic 1729 – 1775.

JOHNSTON informs us that as early as January 10, 1700, four years after the destruction of Fort William Henry by the French and Indians, the board of trade, by order of the king of England, made a report of the conditions of the several forts in his Majesty's plantations. They advised, that for the security of that port and all the country round, and to encourage the people to settle there as formerly, the fort should be rebuilt at Pemaquid.

The authorities both of England and at Boston, recognized the necessity of a strong fort at Pemaquid, but neither wished to incur the expense. Thus for thirty-three years the walls of Fort William Henry lay piled in shapeless ruin.

The white settlers who gradually returned to Pemaquid after the treaty of Utrecht in 1713, encroached upon the lands of the natives. Wars and contention were of frequent occurence. Treaties were made and broken, Gov. Dudley of the Massachusetts colony visited the ruins of Fort William Henry, and he with others strove to have the fort rebuilt, without avail. Conferences were frequently held between the better classes of whites and Indians, showing that the latter were alarmed at the continual encroachments of the English, and the evil influence they exerted by illegal traffic in liquor and other articles. Complaints were made that the truckmaster at St. George, Capt. John Gyles, allowed their young men too much rum and had dealt out to them sour meal and damnified tobacco. They complained that in one instance the English had killed two of their dogs, for only barking at a cow. Their request to the English was, "never to let the trading houses deal in much rum. It wastes the health of our young men, it unfits them to attend prayers. It makes them carry ill, both to your people and their own brethren. This is the mind of our chief men."

These trading or truck houses, as they were often called, were places where the English kept supplies to sell or exchange with the Indians for furs and other articles they might have to dispose of.

The British government, having failed in all this time to induce the Massachusetts Bay Colony to rebuild the fort at Pemaquid, at last resolved to do it. Early in the Spring of 1729, David Dunbar arrived here with a royal commission as Governor, authorizing him to rebuild the fort. He was also appointed surveyor general of the king's woods, which required him to protect the timber of this region, which was suitable for masts, and other purposes for the royal navy.

After rebuilding the fort he named it Fort Frederic in honor of the young prince of Wales, and removed his family here. A detachment of thirty men under proper officers, was sent here to garrison the fort. Aided by a surveyor named Mitchel he laid out magnificent plans for a city about the fort, and three townships, which he named after three English noblemen of the day, Townsend, now Boothbay, Harrington and Walpole, now parts of Bristol. He invited settlers from all parts of the country, promising to supply them land on easy terms.

As an illustration of the hardships endured by some of the first settlers here, soon after the fort was rebuilt, one William Moore, aged seventy-two years, testified that from various causes, "provisions were so scarce among them, the only sustenance this deponent could find for himself and family was clams and water for several weeks together, and he knows not any of the settlers that were not then in the same state, so that when the first child was born in the settlement, not more than three quarts of meal was to be found amongst them all."

Stories of this last fort built, the many stirring and eventful scenes enacted in and about it; the bloody tales of cruel warfare of which Mrs. M. W. Hackelton wrote in her poem entitled "Jamestown of Pemaquid;" those are the tales of adventure; records of tribulation endured by these border settlers in their grim and stubborn struggle for a foothold and new homes in this region. The echoes of their struggles, though now dying out, still linger with us, and few people in all the region but have heard the stories handed down by tradition about Fort Frederic and connected with the settlement here.

They know well that for many years this fort was the haven of refuge and safety, when the wily savage sought vengeance on the white man for encroachment on his land.

I find the names of Moses Young,—— Keent, James Sproul, and —— Reed, who received lots of land lying on the west bank of the Pemaquid River, opposite the fort. They were side by side in the order named, Young's being the northern one. Sproul's lot was the same as that occupied by the late Capt. John Sproul who was his grandson. The latter was accustomed to show in his field some distance east of his house, the foundations of a stone house, erected and occupied by his grandfather; many of their descendants yet reside here. Depredations by the Indians always began when war was declared between France and England, the Indians not even waiting for a formal declaration of war; they often took the inhabitants unawares.

Stories by Capt. Robert Martin and His Sister Miss Margaret.

During one of these unexpected visits to this vicinity by the Indians, they found a mother with her two daughters picking berries some ways east of the fort. On seeing them at a distance they all fled for protection, but the youngest girl, about eleven years old, was overtaken and scalped. The child scalped was thrown on a pile of rocks connected with an outcropping ledge on the east side of McCaffrey's Creek, about one-third the distance from the head to the old burying-ground. Strange to tell, the child's life was saved ; while lying on the rocks her head was in a position to receive the direct rays of the sun, which stanchced the blood, and by that means saved her life, and she was restored to her friends. This is the third case I have ever heard of where a person survived the terrible ordeal of being scalped.

At the foot of Clark's Hill on which the school house now stands, near the house built by Mr. Geo. N. Lewis and since occupied by Mr. Waldo Fossett and Wm. Lewis, with their families, once stood the home of a family named Clark. One day as Mrs. Clark was milking her cows, two Indians surprised her, grabbing her and holding her fast. When they had drank all the milk they wanted, they took her by the arms, one on each side, and began to lead her up the hill. As they were treating her rather roughly, she hung back and indicated that she would follow them if they would let go of her.

She followed them for some distance, gradually dropping back until she was some ways behind, "while they trotted on their tiptoe gate leaning forward" as the captain described it. Turning suddenly, Mrs. Clark fled for her life towards the fort. Perceiving which, one of the Indians raised his gun and fired at her. In those days the women wore what was called "loose gowns and petticoats." The fastening of her lower garment gave way, and tripping over it, she fell to the ground just in time to escape the bullet of the Indian, which grazed along her back, wounding her slightly. She was soon on her feet and off again, and the soldiers from the fort came to her relief, being warned by the report of the Indian's gun.

When the French and Indian War closed by the fall of Quebec in 1759, the usefulness of the fort was ended, which for thirty years had been the haven of refuge, the birth-place, the school and home, of many of the early settlers.

At the Rock Cottage we have a fine portrait of Gen. William North, who was born at this fort in 1755 ; drawn and contributed by Mrs. Fannie Hoyt, formerly Ellis, of this town, to the Pemaquid Improvement Association.

After a few years of peace, in 1762 the great cannon of this fort were carried away to Boston, which had outgrown Pemaquid, and again began the slow decay of this fort, when the people who had used it for protection, scattered away to their homes and different occupations.

I find by the first book of records of the town of Bristol, that about a month after the battle of Lexington, Massachusetts, where the Revolution began April 19, 1775, that the people here became alarmed for their safety and held a town meeting at Capt. John Sproul's house, on May 24, 1775. The first vote recorded, read as follows ; " 1st. Voted that we go down to Pemaquid and tear down the old fort. 2d. Voted that next Tuesday be the day to do it." The settlers had become alarmed by the depredations of the British, as their ships came along this shore before reaching other parts of New England, and as they considered the Yankees rebels, they came on shore and helped themselves to their cattle, sheep and hogs, to obtain supplies of fresh meat.

Two years ago we had a visit from Dr. Perkins of Rockland, Maine, who spent several days in this vicinity to locate the home of his great-grandfather, Mr. Catlin, which he found was on the mainland just west of the bridge which joins it to Rutherford's Island. The following story was told him by his aunt. One day a British officer appeared there with several soldiers and proceeded to take possession of his oxen. Mr. Catlin made objections and tried to prevent the loss of his cattle but it was of no avail. This pompous British officer said to his men, " Take this d—d Yankee rebel's oxen into his parlor and dress them there," and it was done. Such treatment made the people fear that the British would take possession of the fort and use it against them, so they tore down its walls to prevent it.

Several of the older people tell me that when they were children, the old walls stood above the ground in some places eight feet, showing a part of the port holes. Then, I have this testimony by Mr. Calvin C. Robbins, still living. "When I was a boy I worked on this farm with others, for my uncle Samuel Blaisdell, when we had no other employment, he made us work on this wall, taking it down. I have worked on this wall till I wore the skin through on my fingers' ends and made them bleed." "What did you do with the stone?" I inquired. "We had a cart and oxen with us, and after prying them off and loading them, we hauled them down there," (pointing to the river bank) "and dumped them." I suppose a part of those there now, that literally pave the bank and flats at low tide, are a part of the old fort. Said he "My uncle wanted to have a clear yard and view in front of his house and did not care to save the walls as a relic."

The first stone tumbled down have become covered with soil, and the grass having grown over them and the foundation of the wall, it was difficult to convince strangers than even *one* fort had existed here, to say nothing of *four*. Bushes obscured the old Fort Rock, soil and rubbish the castle wall foundations, and we had to dig them out to convince people that they still remained in good condition, the same foundation built by Phips in 1692, over two centuries ago. The mortar they used in the tower castle and front wall thus far excavated, is a puzzle to masons who have examined it. They do not know its composition. Said one mason, "It is better than the cement we have to-day."

CHAPTER XXX

Naval Engagement Off Pemaquid

IN the last war with Great Britain, called the war of 1812, a notable conflict took place on the coast of Maine between the U. S. brig Enterprise and Boxer. The locality of this fierce sea fight was between Pemaquid Point and Monhegan about midway. I spent several days last fall to verify the locality, because it has been claimed by some writers, that the battle occured further west off Portland. With Mr. Alonzo Partridge as assistant, and a compass to determine the course, we climbed Salt Pond hill, which is on the east side of Pemaquid Point. On this height many of the people of the town stood to watch the battle and hailed with joy the victory of the American brig. We found that from our station on the hill a southeast course bore directly toward Monhegan, and over the ocean where the engagement occurred, according to the testimony of many people. That locality is about forty miles east of Portland.

I have met a fisherman who had in his possession a boarding pike of a war vessel brought up by a fish hook from that locality. Another presented me with a human skull obtained in the same manner. For further evidence I visited Rockland, where I met Mrs. Eliza T. Smart, who reached ninety-three years of age in the winter of 1898, and who was doubtless then the only living witness of the conflict. At the time of that war her home was upon Matinicus Island, and all the family witnessed the fight. That island is ten miles east of Monhegan. I was able also to search out the "starboard fore-top-gallant studding sail" of the brig Enterprise, having the name stencilled upon it, and secured a generous piece with the bolt-rope of the sail, both being of different material than that in common use to-day.

The British ship lay at anchor in Johns Bay, near the west shore of the Point, when her antagonist hove in sight, off the Damiscove islands. Her crew at once began preparations for the action. A boat's crew of the Boxer, as aged people tell, were up in Pemaquid harbor, having been sent ashore for a supply of milk from the Old Fort house. They were signalled to return when the American brig was seen. The surgeon and attendants were at Monhegan Island, where they had been called to attend a lad with a broken limb, and were unable to get back to their vessel, as the people held them prisoners.

Mr. Elbridge Wallace, a resident here, informed me that his grandfather, William Curtis, lay hid behind a wood-pile, near the shore where the Boxer lay, and listened to the preparation for the fight, and witnessed the nailing of the flag to the mast-head, by which they showed their determination not to surrender. He afterwards crossed over to the east side of the point to witness the engagement. The vessels did not commence action until past three o'clock in the afternoon, and then the conflict was fierce and sharp at close quarters. Both captains were killed and many men. According to the testimony of one of her seamen, afterwards Capt. William Barnes, the Boxer's hull was so riddled with shot that had the sea been rough she would have filled before her arrival in Portland the next day, where her antagonists took her, and where both captains were buried. The British officer, when ready to stop fighting, shouted through his trumpet his surrender, as the flag could not be hauled down, according to the usual custom.

At the rooms of the Maine Historical Society, in Portland, may be seen the medicine chest of the Boxer, a photograph of a painting of the vessel when in the merchant service two years later, and also several books giving a full description of the engagement.

The name of the American captain was William Barrows, aged 28; his lieutenant, Kerman Waters, and the English captain was Samuel Blithe, aged 29 years. All three were buried side by side on the eastern side of the old cemetery, at Portland.

AN INTERESTING LETTER.

S. E. Norcross sent to the Rockland Free Press the following interesting letter:

Bristol, Maine, June 10th, 1882.

MISS S. E. NORCROSS:

Dear Friend—In the Herald and Record, Damariscotta, of June 1, is published a statement of the battle between the Enterprise and Boxer, during the war of 1812. Permit me to add an incident in the visit of the Boxer to our waters, the day before her capture. The Boxer was cruising off Bristol. Captain John Sproul, with one of the Bristol companies of militia, was quartered in the old Fort Frederic, now called the old Pemaquid Fort, so famous in Indian wars. In Pemaquid harbor, just above the fort, lay a brig at anchor. Saturday the Captain of the Boxer saw her and came into Pemaquid bay, as it is called, within a half mile of the fort, and sent a boat with a flag to the fort, and demanded that they be permitted to board the brig unmolested. As the brig was under a foreign flag—Spanish, I believe—permission was granted. The boat after boarding the brig returned to the Boxer, which had anchored, and she lay at anchor until the forenoon of Sunday, when the Enterprise hove in sight, and the Boxer sailed out around Pemaquid Point, to the eastward of which the battle took place. All living in sight of the ocean saw the battle, and the vessels were in plain sight from the high lands at Round Pond, in Bristol.

We were on a hill a short distance from my father's house, and had an excellent spy-glass. Little could be seen of the vessels while the battle lasted, because of the smoke. We knew the vessels because of the difference in their rig, one being a ship and the other a brig. We could see the boats passing and re-passing, and the Boxer's jibs were hanging under her bowsprit. She was only seven miles distant.

The name of the schooner which burned about twenty sail of vessels off Bristol was the Bream. She was not a privateer, but a government vessel. She did not carry off many, if any of the prizes she captured, but burned them. I saw a number of crews which were landed from the Bream, as they were brought to the back shore, as it is called.

I was born Sept. 9, 1796. Truly yours,

HENRY CHAMBERLAIN.

A SONG OF 1812

Fairly alive with the "spirit of 1812" is the ballad herewith printed. For its contribution we have to thank H. W. Bryant, who discovered the militant song of years agone in a niche of his curio storehouse, which is so universally resorted to by those delving into the past.—*Argus.*

YE PARLIAMENT OF ENGLAND

Ye Parliament of England,
  You Lords and Commons, too,
Consider well what you're about
  And what you're going to do;
You're now to fight with Yankees,
  I'm sure you'll rue the day
You roused the Sons of Liberty
  In Nortn America.

You first confined our commerce
  And said our ships shant trade;
You next impressed our seamen
  And used them as your slaves;
You then insulted Rodgers
  While ploughing on the main,
And had we not declared war
  You'd have done it o'er again.

You thot our frigates were but feg,
And Yankees could not fight,
Until brave Hull your Guerriere took
And banished her from your sight;
The Wasp then took your Frolic,
We'll nothing say to that,
The Poictiers being of the line
Of course she took her back.

Then next your Macedoninn,
No finer ship could swim,
Decatur took her gilt work off
And then he sent her in.
The Java by a Yankee ship
Was sunk, you all must know;
The Peacock, fine in all her plume,
By Lawrence down did go.

Then next you sent your Boxer,
To box us all about,
But we had an "enterprising" brig
That beat your Boxer out;
We boxed her up to Portland,
And moored her off the town,
To show the Sons of Liberty
The Boxer of renown.

Then next upon Lake Erie,
Where Perry had some fun,
You own he beat your naval force,
And caused them for to run.
This was to you a sore defeat,
The like n'er known before—
Your British squadron beat complete—
Some took, some run ashore.

There's Rodgers, in the President,
Will burn, sink and destroy;
The Congress on the Brazil coast
Your commerce will annoy;
The Essex in the South seas,
Will put out all your lights;
The flag she waves at her mast-head—
"Free trade and sailors' rights."

Lament, ye sons of Britian,
  For distant is the day
When you'll regain by British force
  What you've lost in America.
Go tell your King and Parliament,
  By all the world 'tis known,
That British force by sea and land
  By Yankees is o'erthrown.

Use every endeavor
  And strive to make peace,
For Yankee ships are building fast
  Their navy to increase;
They will enforce their commerce,
  The laws by Heaven were made
That Yankee ships in time of peace
  To any port may trade.

CHAPTER XXXI

The Pemaquid Improvement Association

THE first meeting of the Association was held October 31, 1893, at the home of Mrs. Jennie Partridge, in the room then occupied as a Post Office. Following are the names of those who attended at that time:

George N. Lewis	J. Henry Cartland
Henry C. Partridge	Lorenzo D. McLain
Albert C. Sproul	Lincoln J. Partridge
George D. Tarr	Augustus McLain

I spent a good part of the winter traveling on foot over this town and Bremen, once a part of Bristol. I succeeded in accumulating nearly $200, and with that amount and other contributions by visitors interested, we secured enough to unearth the foundation walls of the Castle, which we found to be eight feet high, and the front walls of the fort, which were one hundred and fifty feet long and six feet thick.

This account, with the accompanying cuts, will give one an idea how the foundation walls and buried relics here were first brought to light.

The following report was published Jan. 11, 1894, in the Pemaquid Messenger.

Names of those who have paid one dollar and more, and those who have pledged themselves to pay the sum set against their names, over that portion of the town thus far canvassed, to assist this Association, in connection with the Monumental Association, to unearth, preserve and restore the ancient landmarks of note, at this place.

It is but justice to say that I have found the people of Bristol, thus far, more interested than I expected to. Many who have not felt able to spare the money this winter, promise to help the movement along in the spring ; some with money and others with labor. All can see that if carried on this work will eventually benefit every citizen who is interested in the moral or intellectual welfare of our town and State.

This list has been published before completing the canvass of the town, or either village thoroughly, to show people that we are in earnest about this matter, and we trust that every citizen of the town and all others interested will notify their friends, wherever located, of this movement, and encourage them to send us funds to carry on this work so long neglected. They can well realize that one small association, village or town, cannot carry on this work to perfection unless others aid us with money.

The illustrations accompanying this account will convey some idea of what has been done. The first shows how it looked after over half the bushes and rubbish which hid it from view were cleared away. The second shows a small part of the foundation of the old castle wall which had been hidden by the destruction of that above it—the precaution of the citizens at the opening of the Revolution. The top of the wall had been tumbled down, burying eight feet of the foundation. When we began work it was difficult to convince people that even one fort had been erected and destroyed here, to say nothing of four, one of which cost nearly £20,000. The next cut shows how it looked until the State re-built the Castle in 1907–8. The two white towers were constructed of the stone which composed the upper part of the castle that has been twice built up and twice destroyed. Between these towers was a wooden structure which answered for a temporary museum, where some of the relics discovered were placed on exhibition. The very stones used in those towers are of historic interest, and have been saved in close proxlmity to the foundations of the old castle so as to be replaced for the third time.

What more unique or appropriate monument could ever be rebuilt here? It would be a relic of colonial days unsurpassed, and to be compared with those seen in England and Germany to-day; a tower of observation overlooking the archipelago of Pemaquid, the river, bay and ocean, with their panoramic view of ships not inferior to any along our New England shores. Its walls would enclose rooms for a fire-proof museum where showcases can be placed to contain the cannon balls, bomb shells and other choice relics which are brought to light from beneath the soil of this historic place. Its inner walls should be decorated with the artist's canvas covered with paintings of the ships of war and peace and the noble men that once made old Pemaquid famous. Within its walls should be a library, where the scattered records of its history might be gathered and preserved, studied and enjoyed by the children of our old commonwealth and all others interested. Slowly but persistently this small organization has carried on the work of gathering history and unearthing the buried ruins of this place. We are now in need of funds to complete the excavations of the front wall which was begun in the fall of 1893. We will then be able to show all visitors indisputable evidence of the solid structure built here long ago. We were rewarded by finding seventeen cannon balls ranging from three and one-half to seventeen and three-quarter pounds, and a barrel of choice relics near the wall thus far excavated. Our appeal is particularly to the natives of old Maine, wherever located, who have a pride in her past and present history. Here, where civilization began in New England, a monument should be erected worthy of our State and nation. We now await the financial aid of tbose who have the welare of the rising generation at heart, and trust our past record of work done here will secure us the aid and confidence of those who desire this work go on. We may then be able to add more laurels to those already won by the old Pine Tree State, for being the first place where important events transpired in our country, beside the first to greet the morning sun.

CHAPTER XXXII

BRISTOL HISTORY

Important Dates in Bristol and Pemaquid History

1605 Capt. Geo. Waymouth visits the Maine coast and captures five Pemaquid Indians.

1607, August 8 and 10. Pemaquid is visited by Captain Popham's Colony.

1614 Capt. John Smith visits Monhegan and Pemaquid,

1621 Charter issued by Council of Plymouth to John Pierce et als. (Pemaquid Patent.)

1625 John Brown purchases land of Indians—Capt. John Samorset and Unongoit—including Muscongus, or Loud's Island.

1626 Alderman Aldsworth and Gyles Elbridge of Bristol, England, purchase Pemaquid Patent.

1631 Fort Pemaquid erected by Aldsworth and Eldridge.

1632 Fort plundered by Dixie Bull, a pirate.

1635 The "Angel Gabriel" destroyed at Pemaquid by a big storm.

1664 King Charles 2d granted this territory to his brother, the Duke of York, afterward James 2d.

1667 Fort Charles erected by Gov. Andros of New York.

1674 Devonshire County organized.

1676 All settlements destroyed by Penobscot Indians.

1686 Jurisdiction ceded to Massachusetts.

1689 Fort and settlement destroyed by Indians.

1692 Fort Wm. Henry built by Gov. Phips, 28 guns mounted.

1696 Pemaquid, "the strongest fastness of the British in North America," captured by French and Indians under "Castine."

1729 Gov. David Dunbar arrives; fort re-built and named Fort Frederic; Townsend, Harrington and Walpole surveyed and lotted out.

1745–48 Fifth Indian war, many depredations committed at Pemaquid, Walpole and other settlements.

1757 Nicholas Davidson becomes sole proprietor of Pemaquid Patent.

1764 Population about 200.

1765 First act of incorporation passed, and town named Bristol, for Bristol, England. Town organized Dec. 4th.

1766 Second act, including Broad Cove, passed.

1775 Wm. Jones sent to Legislature, the first Representative from Bristol.

1775 Fort demolished by town of Bristol.

1800 Walpole Post Office established—the first in Bristol.

1813 The British brig Boxer captured by the Enterprise, off Pemaquid Point, near Monhegan.

1814 Engagement between the British from the frigate Maidstone and 100 men of Pemaquid, under Capt. Sproul.

1824 Lighthouse erected at Pemaquid Point.

1828 Bremen incorporated, Bristol Mills Post Office established.

1835 Pemaquid Falls P. O. established.

1847 Damariscotta incorporated.

1850 Round Pond Post Office established.

1861–65 337 men sent to the Union Army.

1863 South Bristol Post Office established on Rutherford's Island.

Before the Post Office was established at New Harbor, Mr. N. J. Hanna, when a boy of about nine years of age, was employed to bring the mail from Pemaquid Falls, a distance of about three miles. It came but once a week then, and his compensation for carrying it and traveling six miles was fifty cents.

About 1878 Alex. H. Brackett was the first Postmaster appointed by the Government, N. J. Hanna second, Edward W. Fossett third, Charles T. Poland fourth, and Mertland Carroll fifth, now serving—1915.

July 1, 1890, the Post Office at Pemaquid Beach was established, with Jennie E. Lewis, Postmaster, Nathan George Lewis Assistant, and J. H. Cartland, Clerk. The first daily paper sold there was the Boston Herald. Next to hold the office was Winnie McLain, then Dorcas Gray, and now by Wilda E. Sproul. Both the New Harbor and Pemaquid Beach offices are Money Order offices, and receive the mail twice each day in summer.

Report of the Superintendent of Schools for 1914

To the Board of Education, and people of Bristol:—It is with pleasure that I comply with the duty of submitting to you my 3rd annual report of the schools of Bristol.

At the annual spring election, held Mar. 10th, 1913, Mr. J. E. Nichols was elected a member of the Board of Education for three years, and Mr. A. C. Fossett for two years.

The Board met at Round Pond, Mar. 13th, and organized with the choice of H. G. Poole as chairman, and the reappointment of Norris A. Miller as Superintendent of Schools.

There is a general awakening in the interest of the schools in most of the towns of the State, and I believe that Bristol is in line with this progressive movement. There is no question but parents and citizens generally are taking more interest in the schools than ever before, which is proven by the visits of the parents to the schools, more ready compliance to the school rules, and more help to the teachers. Another proof is a larger registration of scholars and a better attendance than heretofore. The Course of Study by grades has proven to be one of the greatest blessings to our schools, for it has created an interest among the pupils for promotion from grade to grade, the completion of the Grammar school work and admission to the High School. It is very pleasing to note that no cases of contagious diseases have appeared in our schools during the school year and the general health of the pupils and teachers has been excellent. While I am satisfied that our schools are on an equality with schools of other towns, yet they are open for improvement.

Probably no town in Lincoln County has better school Buildings (taken as a whole) than Bristol. The writer in visiting the towns in the County paid particular attention to school property. While our buildings are among the best, we are sadly in need of play grounds for the children. In a majority of our schools the children are obliged to play in the road, causing great danger to themselves and inconvenience to the public. The town should take some action in the near future for the enlargement of our school grounds.

In my 1912–13 report I cited the excellent work the school was doing, the interest manifested on the part of the student body, parents and citizens, the crowded condition of the school at that time and asked the citizens for an appropriation for the enlargement of the building.

This the voters very generously accorded, and we have to-day a large, and well proportioned building, with commodious rooms well lighted, heated, and ventilated, and which is an honor to the town and State. Today there are enrolled in this school, eighty students, manifesting that same interest as heretofore. A business or Commercial Course has been added to the curriculm, thus giving our boys and girls a chance to secure a business education at home. Three courses of study are now provided, viz: College preparatory, English, and Commercial.

Mr. V. H. Robinson, the principal, has been connected with the school for six years, and during this time under his tact and ability, it has grown from a small body of students to its present size, and excellent condition.

Respectfully submitted, NORRIS A. MILLER.

This school opened in the Fall in its new addition to Lincoln School building. The main room will seat 30 pupils, and is attractive, well lighted, and ventilated. When needed, a part of the cloak room can be used for laboratory work. The school opened with 13 students under the instruction of Mr. Farren, who is proving himself an excellent teacher. During my visit to the school, I noted much interest manifested by the pupils and saw some excellent work. The school is now small, but if continued in a few years, it will probably reach a much larger attendance.

The following letter from Mrs. Lois M. Geyer, was furnished me recently, giving the names of pastors of the Methodist Episcopal Church.

New Harbor, Me. Nov. 10th 1914

MR. J. H. CARTLAND :

Dear Sir—I hereby send you a list of the Pastors of the Methodist Episcopal Church, since its organization in 1848, until the present time. The Parsonage was at Bristol Mills until 1888, when it was moved to Pemaquid. Pemaquid and New Harbor were then classed as one.

There were a few years I think we had no stationed Pastor, but were supplied by local preachers. Once in particular after the Old Union Church was built in 1856, we had no pastor sent us for a year, but were supplied by Paris Rowell, who was a local Preacher, and back in my girlhood days by Hiram Murphy, who lived in town.

If there is any other information I can give you, I will be glad to do it. Hoping I have made this plain, I remain,

Yours respectfully, LOIS M. GEYER

The following is the Pastoral record of Bristol, of which Pemaquid forms the South end. 1848–49 Seth H. Beale, '49 Edwin A. Helmerhausen, '50 Benjamin Bryant, '51 Cyrus Phenix, '52 William H. Crawford, '53–54 Geo. D. Strout, '55 Geo. G. Winslow, '56 True P. Adams, '57–58 Benj. F. Sprague '59–60 Nathan Webb, '61 Josiah I. Brown, '62 Wm. H. Crawford, '63 Phineas Higgins, '64 James Hartford, '65 Alfred S. Adams, '67 Paris Rowell, '69 Josiah Bean, '70 Joseph King, '73–74 Nathan Webb, '75 Edmund H. Tunnicliffe, '76 no Pastor, '77–78–79 John P. Siminton, '80 Frank D. Hondy, '81–82–83 Moses G. Prescott, '84–85–86 Emery Glidden, '87 Wilbur F. Chase, '88 Wm. H. Faroat. For Pemaquid and New Harbor, '89 Vinal E. Hill, '90–91 Preston A. Smith, '92 Melvin S. Preble, '93–94–95–96 Jas. H. Morelen, '97–98 Carl E Petersen, '1899–1905 Arthur Lockhart, '05–06 Frank W. Brooks, '06–10 Charles F, Beebee, '10–12 Edward J. Webber, '12–14 C. Jasper Irwin, '14 Allan W. Constantine.

In 1772 Bristol was erected into three Parishes, viz.: Walpole, Harrington and Broad Cove. A meeting house was soon after erected in each Parish. Rev. Alexander McLean a Presbyterian, became pastor in 1772 and remained until 1795, died in 1808.

The Churches of to-day at Bristol are 9, and two chapels, one at West Bristol and one at South Bristol, Old Walpole built in 1772, Harrington near Pemaquid Falls, Round Pond two, Methodist and Universalist; Bristol Mills two, Congregational and Methodist; Pemaquid Falls, Methodist, built 1837; New Harbor two, Methodist and Union.

The first Church built at New Harbor was a Union church built at the expense of Mr. Alex. G. Poland, and contained fifty-eight pews, though only about half were ever sold. He also owned the land on which it was located. This was occupied by many Pastors of different denominations, people of any denomination having the right to speak there. Mr. Wm. Hackelton and Deacon Wm. Foster of Rockport, Mass., are remembered as teachers in the Sabbath Schools. The church was destroyed by fire after many years of service, and another built by the people of New Harbor and the surrounding villages, with some outside assistance by the Methodist Episcopal Society.

The second Church built at New Harbor in 1885 was burned on Jan. 1st. 1911. The building committee were Capt. Geo. Johnston, N. J. Hanna and Alex. G. Poland. A remarkable record was made by citizens of the surrounding villages, and some assistance by people who were non-residents, in having a new and more mordern church erected, all paid for, and dedicated on Nov. 11th, 1914, in less than one year.

This society is joined with the one at Pemaquid Falls. The People of Pemaquid and Long Cove attend Church there, it being the most central point for all.

Soldiers of the Civil War

Following are the names of the soldiers who enlisted during the Civil War—1861 to 1865.

Edwin D. Bailey
Harvey Bearce, Corp.
David Bryant, Jr., Sergt.
Linsdale Burnham
Green Burns
Albert S. Clark, Surgeon
J. S. Clark
Orvill H. Clark, Corp.
John T. Dyer
Arnold B. Erskine, Corp.
Jas. H. Erskine
Jas. D. Erskine, Lieut.
Chas. W. Ford, Lieut.
Emery H. Ford
Ambrose H. Foster
Isaac W. Foster
Lewis S. Golloup
Timothy F. Gowdy
Henry G. Gowdy
Donald M. Hastings
Phillip Hatch
Wm. M. Herbert, Sergt.

John W. Hyson, Jr.
Cyrus F. Jones
Samuel Jones
Solomon Lain
Thaddeus Little, Adjutant
Frank H. Lailer
Edw. D. McClain
Parker Mears
Jos. E. Mears
Benjamin Quimby
Bedfield Sproul
Chas. E. Sproul
Chas. M. Thompson
Lucius B. Varney
Nath. Wentworth
Nathaniel Barker
Arad Barker, Corp.
Briggs G. Besse
John M. Bryant, Corp.
Francis A. Brackett
Josiah J. Brown, Chap.
Elbridge R. Bryant, Sergt.
Timothy F. Brown
Orin Carter
Geo. B. Caswell
Levi Cudworth
Austin Curtis
Alvin Cutler
Andrew J. Erskine, Capt.
Lemuel Erskine
Geo. T. Emerson
John H. Erskine
Wilson T. Erskine
John Ervine
Jos. B. Fitch, Capt.
Atwood Fitch, Lieut.
Samuel H. Fitch, Corp.
John H. Ford
Thomas H. Fossett
Augustus H. Ford, Sergt.
Samuel L. Foster
Thomas A. Foster
Orin I. Gaul, Musician
John Goudy
Albert Hatch
Enoch Hatch
Robert Hanley
Lyman Hanna
Robert Henry
Albert Herbert
Nathan C. Hodgdon
Edward A. Humphrey
Abel C. Huston, Sergt.
Elbridge R. Huston
Henry C. Huston
David Hysom
Robert S. Hysom
Zebard F. Hysom
John E. Johnston
William J. Kelsey
Alonzo Lawton
Daniel W. Little
Thomas C. Little
Patrick Mann, Corp.
John J. McIntyre
Ruben R. McFarland
John McIntyre
Wm. H. McIntyre
Wm. D. Kirn
Jas. N. Myers

Wm. Nash
Jas. E. Nichols, Com. Sergt.
Jos. Odlam
Geo. Palmer
Stephen Palmer
Freeman Peasley, Corp.
John Pool Jr.
Julian B. Perkins
Geo. W. Prentis
Enoch O. Richards
Montgomery Richards
Calvin C. Rogers, Sergt.
Marion Simmons
Ephraim Stevens
David P. Sproul
August M. Sproul, Corp.
Simeon Tarr
Bradford Thompson
Samuel F. Tarr
Everett A. Wentworth
Wilson J. Yates
Enoch Wentworth
Stanley C. Alley, Corp.
Henry H. Goudy
John Goudy
Charles G. Kenney
Henry H. Webber
Geo. H. M. Barrett
Franklin H. Bell
Wesley A. Bell
Patrick Burns
John Conner
Henry B. Richards
Chas. H. Robinson
Wesley Scott
Richard H. Short
Franklin B. Tarr
John Tyler
John Welch
Ambrose Foster
John M. Gamage
Jos. Hanscomb
John McManus
Freeman Peasley, Corp.
Albert L. Wiles
Edwin W. Merrill
Gilbert P. Brown
Abdon Davis
Gilbert Hammond
John A. Johnson
Thomas King
Lander M. Reeves
Wilmot Russel
Thomas Wentworth
Joseph Burns
Van B. Fountain
Chas. Johnson
Lavoir Mansen
Jas. Rice
Jos. W. Sproul
Jos. Willet
Liman Curtis
Marcus A. Hannah
Geo. W. Huston
Richard Keyes
Wm. P. Perley
Alonzo Richards
Wm. E. Thompson

Foreign Enlistments

Wm. Davis

Jas. Erskine
Joshua Gammage
Chas. Hanley
John Martin
Llewellyn McLain
Chas. Swain
Jacob Day
Chas. E. Foster
Jas. Gray
Wm. Lane
Augustus McLain
Elliot Pierce
Geo. H. Andrew
Lyman Curtis, Boston
John Chamberlain, N. Y. St.
Daniel Mason R. I.
Leander McFarland
SilasPenniman, Ohio
Fred' k Creamer, Waldoboro
Randall E. Humphrey, Corp.
M.V. B. Robinson, Lewiston
Robert Brackett, Portland
Lewis L. Walker
Calvin C. Robbins

CHAPTER XXXIII

MUSCONGUS ISLAND HISTORY

The island known as Muscongus or Louds Island, and earlier as Samoset's Island, is of much historical interest. Here, it is said, the noted Indian chief Samoset, held his headquarters, and the early Indian Cemetery, located near the northern end of the island, is said to be his final resting place.

The Island is about three miles long, with average width of one mile, and is shaped to resemble a miniature South America. A good Harbor indents the eastern coast line ground, around which are clustered several fishermen's homes. Marsh Island, which shelters the harbor (bearing the same name) is the home of one family. The residents are chiefly fishermen, although the island contains some good farms.

Alexander Gould, a son in law of John Brown, was probably the first white settler, coming here around 1650. William Loud, an English naval Officer, together with one Bishop, came here about the middle of the 18th century. Wm. Loud located in the north-east end of the island. He was born around 1710, died about 1800. His son, Wm. Solomon Loud, born about 1740, died about 1820, was the father of Samuel, William and Roberts. Samuel moved to Round Pond, and William to Orrington. Roberts remained on the island and is the ancestor of many of the present families.

Wm. Carter, great grand father of the present generation, and Wm. Carter, Jr., were the first of this name to live here. They were of Scottish descent, but born in England. John L. Carter, father of Robert, was born here Oct. 10th, 1799. When returning from meteing with others he saw clearly the famous battle between the Boxer and Enterprise, which was fought between Pemaquid and Monhegan. Robert has long been a leading man in managing the island's affairs.

The Poland family is of English Origin. Leonard Poland came from Massachusetts shortly after the Revolution, and is said to be the only man of Muscongus Island who saw service in the war for Indpendence. He enlisted at the age of fourteen, and when he arrived here, he settled on Marsh Island, and now lies buried in the Island Cemetery.

The Island enjoys a peculiar political setting inasmuch as it has no government whatever, and pays no allegiance to a sovereign power. It is classified as a part of Lincoln County, and has always remained true to the Union when approached properly. Its people cast no vote, and pay no taxes. The last vote cast by the Islanders was at Lincoln's first election, when they voted with Bristol. Their vote was, with one exception, democratic and carried the town democratic. The vote was then counted, and their vote thrown out, leaving Bristol a republican majority.

Up to this time taxes had been paid in the town of Bristol. The only local expense was the support of schools, which was met by receipts paid by the New London fishermen, who came there each spring for lobsters, and bought the privilege of fishing there. After the trouble with Bristol, the Islanders having been deprived of their suffrage, upon advice of several lawyers, refused to pay taxes, saying, "We are willing to support the United States, but refuse to help Bristol."

During the Civil War Bristol made a draft of her citizens, including the islanders, and by some accident an unequally large percentage fell to the Islanders. Nine men from a possible forty-five were drawn to fill Bristol's quota. The men refused to honor such a draft. When an officer landed to summons them he was met by a fusilade of boiled potatoes from the hands of an indignant matron, and driven from the Island. Citizens of the islands then employed David Chamberlain, Esq., to visit the authorities at Augusta to learn their legal rights and duties in the matter, and found Bristol had no right to draft them. They then met a proportional draft among their own citizens. John Loud, John Thompson, and Henry McGray were drafted and bought substitutes. Later the residents bought other substitues for drafted men. No citizen enlisted.

Frederick Turner, a homoeopathic doctor, was the only resident practicing physician. He was an Englishman who came here from Bangor before the war.

The Baptist Church was organized about 1794; Wm. Jones, John Murphy, and Robert Oram were early deacons. Sylvanus P. Low came in the spring of 1861. Elder Edw. Dunbar sometimes preached here, but Elder Edw. Turner was probably the first established pastor. Revs. Enos Trask, Wentworth Weeks, Ring, Flagg, Chas. E. Hawes, Chisam and Pillsbury, were later preachers. Rev. Fred Farnham was the last Pastor.

The Muscongus Bethel Church (Cogregational), is a branch of the Portland Bethel, and was organized Feb. 10th, 1897. Rev. H. J. Allen was pastor three years. Zenas Hoffses and Constantine Carter were the first deacons. John Carter is now deacon, and Joseph Carter clerk. A Christian Endeavor Society holds regular services, and a Sabbath School is maintained.

The earliest school house was built of rough stones. This was replaced by the old brick house, and that in turn by the present wooden structure about thirty years ago. The occasion of a flag raising about fifteen years ago, was an event of much interest and largely attended. An address was delivered by R. H. Oram of Bristol. The Island school is well maintained by the payment of a certain sum for each pupil in attendance by their parents. Three terms are held each year with an average attendance of about eighteen scholars. The management is vested with a school agent chosen each year.

INDEX

PAGE

Alewives and other migratory Fish and Birds--14, 52
Archibald, Capt. Issac ----22
Archangel, first ship lost on N. E. shores, 1635------24
Adams, on Civilization----53
American Antiquarian So.-67
Aldsworth, deed of land---67
Angel Gabriel, wreck of---69
Acadia, Pemaquid a part --35
Andros, Gov. Sir Redmond his Proclamation----80, 83
Ambrose, Capt., his sailors and loss of ship --------96
Bristol, name derived------8
Bristol History-----------208
Baron de Castine ----14, 182
Boothbay, East -----------14
Boothbay Harbor 12,15, 52, 54
Brick-making ------------15
Birch Island ------------24
Beaver Island --------29, 30
Bashaba, or King of the Indians-----------------36
Berries, abundance -------39
Baxter, address by----48, 105
Bradford, Gov., sends food for Pilgrims-----------54
Brown, John, Richard ----58
Bailey, separation from wife by terrors of the sea ----72
Baker, Mrs. Martha A.----72
Blaisdell, John ----------97
Blaisdell, Samuel P.-----110
Blacksmith Shops-------132
Burying yard, old 26, 148,150
Boxer and Enterprise ----105

PAGE

Bradford, Gov., complaints against Pemaquid -------74
Brockholls, Capt. Anthony 81
Brackett, Col. Thom--97, 125
Thos., Jack a slave-----98
Bremen ----------------98
Blockhouse, at Wiscasset --56
Bombshells ---------99, 104
first used, Pemaquid---182
Christmas Cove-------16, 17
Curtis, Laforest----------19
Cooking under difficulties--20
City of Portland, steamer--23
Chamberlain, H. H., sch.--23
Clark, William ----------28
Claims, Spain and Portugal 34
Cross, set up on Georges Is. 86
at Thomaston-----------41
Charles, Prince, of England 49
Cellars, old----------52, 115
Codfish, at Boston and Pemaquid -------------39, 56
Cox and Newman, signers of first Deed-----------60
Cape Newagen-----------65
Cattle and other animals --70
Cogswell. John, a London merchant -------------70
Cattle, price of, 1636------75
Cannon, French and English-------------103, 106
Chamberlain, J. L.------105
Cartland, Jacob Alonzo --112
Caché, the -------------127
Chadwick, Frank--------144
Chub, Pasco, commander of the fort-------------183

PAGE

Clark, Mrs. escape Indians 196
Columbus ---------------- 90
Castle, view from 92, 102, 106
Caquina, where found ----- 95
Carty, John -------------- 97
Damariscotta, river and village --------------- 12, 16
Damiscove ------------ 13, 52
DeIberville ------------- 100
Dunbar, David ----------- 15
Dolliver, Charles A. ------ 22
Dunham, Isaac and Dr. V. B. 22
Davenport, Albert -------- 27
Deed, first ex. in America 58-9
Drown ------------------ -67
D'Aulney, death of ------- 77
Dickey, Col. ------------- 91
Davis, Capt. Wm. --------- 94
Dunbar, Col. David ------ 108
Dodge, Asa J. ----------- 113
Duck, a remarkable ------ 114
Documents, French ------- 83
Enterprise, Steamer ------ 14
Edmands, Geo, F., loss of -- 25
Earthy, John ------------- 62
Elbridge, Gyles ------ 67, 68
Edgemere, Hotel --------- 96
Erskine, Col. Jas. -------- 110
Friends, or Quakers ------ 15
Fort Island -------------- 15
Frigates of War --------- 30
Fish, found in abundance -- 39
  Hatchery, Government -- 27
French, first colony in 1604 48
Fort, plan of, found in Spain 48
  Frederic, 1729-'75 ---- 193
  Vote to destroy -------- 197
  Rock ----------------- 92
  Wm. Henry & Frederic 105
  House or mansion 108, 111
  Charles, soldiers -- 164, 168
  Wm. Henry ---- 175, 178-9

PAGE

Forts Farley and Frederic -- 55
Fitch, Joseph B. ---- 117, 124
Fossett, Capt. ----------- 129
Fortifications ----------- 161
Fishermen, English ------ 13
Gamage, Nelson ---------- 15
  Fanny ----------------- 25
Geyer, Capt. Chas. -------- 20
Greenleaf, Capt. Geo. ---- 27
Gorges, Sir Fernando -- 40, 57
Gilbert, Capt. ----------- 46
Giles, Elbridge and Thomas 85
  160, 165, 170
Gibbons ----------------- 77
Gould, Nathan ---------- 124
Gravestones, old -------- 153
Heron Island, outer, inner 13
Holly Inn --------------- 18
Holmes, E. C. ----------- 18
Humphrey, Capt. Wm. S. -21
Harvey, Capt. Isaac ------ 27
Hotel Waneta ----------- 30
History of Pemaquid, Historical Society --------- 32
Historical Tablet --------- 43
Hunt, his treachery ------ 65
Haines, Deacon ------ 14, 72
Hackelton, Mrs. Maria ---- 91
Horsford, Cynthia -------- 93
Hancock, John ---------- 98
House, the Old Fort ------ 100
Higiman, Grace, prisoner by the Indians -------- 169
Introduction ------------ 5
Ice Cutting -------------- 15
Islands of Pemaquid ------ 18
Indians, traffic with 37—40, 62
  Exhibit of at England -- 45
  Narragansett ---------- 80
  Massacre at the Falls -- 171
  Doctor, Big Thunder -- 179
  Mickmack ------------- 77

PAGE

Isle of Shoals............70
John, Island, Bay and River
25, 28, 29
Jewel of Artes...........43
Johnson, Prof. John......67
Capt. Geo..............90
Jamestown...............81
King Phillip, 1676 13
War of..................79
King, cottages of 27
Kennedy, Capt. Alexander 27
Kings of France and England, contention....34, 35
Kelley, John P............96
LaTour, Chas. 75
Linnekin's Bay, attractions 12
Lewis, John..............23
Lobster Pounds 27
London Comp'y, Lord Chief Justice, etc.............45
Levett, his testimony.....65
LeTour 75, 77. 88
Liquor Traffic, early laws..87
Lewis, Nathan and Geo. N.
93, 94
Lobsters 106
May-flowers 11
Medocawondo, Indian Chf.170
House.................14
McFarland. E.............15
Mussel and Oyster Shells..18
Monhegan, origin of name.21
Visit of Capt. Waymouth
vegetation, etc.35, 36, 52
Machete, or Spanish cane knife 93
Museum 100
Magnolia, Cotton Mather 101
Magazine...............106
Maine Historical Society, interesting meeting 126,156
Muscongus Island 218

PAGE

McLain, Wm., Harold, A. D., Capt. Melville, L.D. Parson Alexander...19, 28
93, 112, 122, 157
Marr, C. E.............22, 135
Miles, Samuel S. 28
McFarland, Addison, shop 27
Maps, Ft. Popham,in Spain 32
English, French, Spanish and Portuguese 50
Monuments, educational ..55
Massasoit, treaty with Pilgrims 65
Mather, Rev. Richard, Increase and Cotton70, 72,100
Naval battle, relics, etc...199
Newport,ship.............11
Norsemen 17
North, of Augusta and Pemaquid 28
Nahanada 47,61,107,108,110
New Harbor 51
North, Gen. William 105
Nichols, Capt. John, wife 105
Oyster, shell heaps....10, 16
Oram, Capt. Robert 25
Oliver...................62
Pilgrims 63
Patent, the 67, 71
Phips, Sir William 177
Paintings, Books, etc. 100,102
Pell, Howland...........100
Portland, inhabitants all killed 1690 103
Popham, Sir John.........45
Capt. and Gilbert, visit Pemaquid 47
Sir Francis New Harbor 49
Pilgrims at Cape Ann..54, 55
Proclamation by Gov. Andrews 83
Plymouth, supplies gone 53, 56

PAGE

Pemaquid, at this time----12
Pavings ----------95, 119
Government ----------81
Rivers------------92, 100
Officers appointed ------85
Boundaries------12, 75, 79
Point Light ----------22
Improvement Association 29
First Settled ----------30
Old records------------32
Called St Johns town --49
Early Traffie ----------51
Alewive industry ------52
The Metropolis --------86
Relics ------90, 93, 105-6
Rosier's account of visit of Waymouth--------34
Siege, British outfit----187
Pipe manufacturing----134
Partridge, J. W. 22, 29, 110-11
Jabob ------------98, 99
Pool, Capt. Willard ------23
Porgies, or Menhaden ----26
Factories---------------30
Port Royal --------------35
Plymouth Co. --------45, 53
Paul, Mrs.---------------107
Quakers, the meeting-house 98
Resorts, Maine coast------9
Rock of Pemaquid--------10
Race, Capt. Alfred--------14
Rutherford's Island----15, 24
Rutherford, Rev. Robert--15
Rice Brothers-------------15
Rowe, Capt. Seth --------27
Russell, Mrs. Annie York 29, 96, 100
Relics, of New Harbor ----52
of early date-----------159
Rhinelander, T. J. Oakley 105
Robbins, Calvin C. ------110

PAGE

Summit House ----------15
Shipbuilding, Damariscotta 16
Shipley, John B., his early records --------------16
Summer Cottages of the lobster fishermen ----------18
Sproul, Henry---------18, 19
Stephens, Ralph-----------19
Sewall, R. K.-------------21
Smith, Capt. John 22, 32, 49, 50
St. Croix River ----------35
St. Georges Islands--------36
Shurte, Abram 52, 60, 62, 67
Shalop, Sparrow-----------53
Storms, great, of 1624, '35 69
Samosett ----------59, 63-6
Sharp, Thos. -------------85
St. Augustin -------------95
Summer visitors-----------97
Ships, Angel Gabriel and James ---------------128
Comparison, arrival, etc. 45
Showels ---------------145
Steamers ----------------10
Thorpe Brothers-----------17
Thread of Life------------28
Tercentenary, The, of first landing on N.E. shores--48
Tablet, on Kennebcc -----48
Thornton, J. Wingate ----57
Thayer, Rev. Henry O. --183
Tibbetts, Chas. F., son Wm. 96
Viking, ship -------------16
Virginia, ship -----------48
Vessels granted passes ----88
old-------------137, 139
Witch Island-------------26
Whales--------------39, 49
Winslow, Kanelm, Phœbe-54
Washington, Gen.---------55
Wharves, old --141, 142, 144

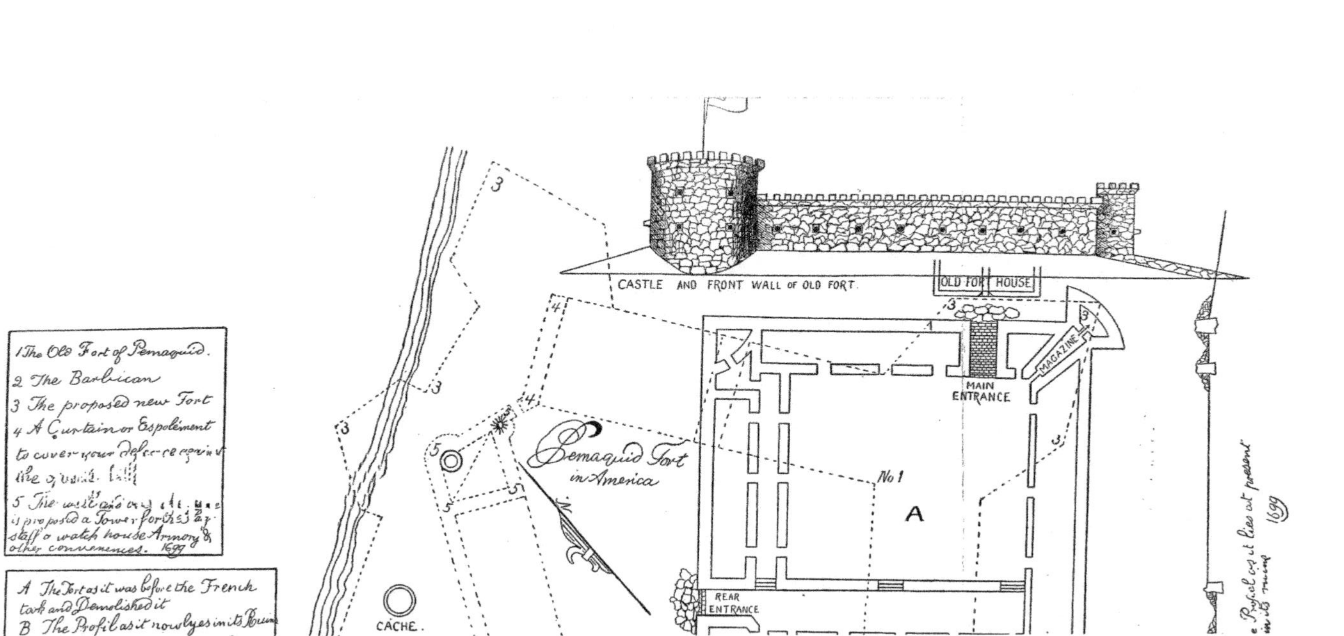

CASTLE AND FRONT WALL OF OLD FORT.
OLD FORT HOUSE
MAGAZINE
MAIN ENTRANCE
REAR ENTRANCE
A
No 1
CACHE.
Pemaquid Fort in America
1 The Old Fort of Pemaquid.
2 The Barbican
3 The proposed new Fort
4 A Curtain or Espolément
5 ... is proposed a Tower for the flag staff a watch house Armory & other conveniences. 1699
A The Fort as it was before the French took and Demolished it
B The Profil as it now lyes in its Ruins
1699

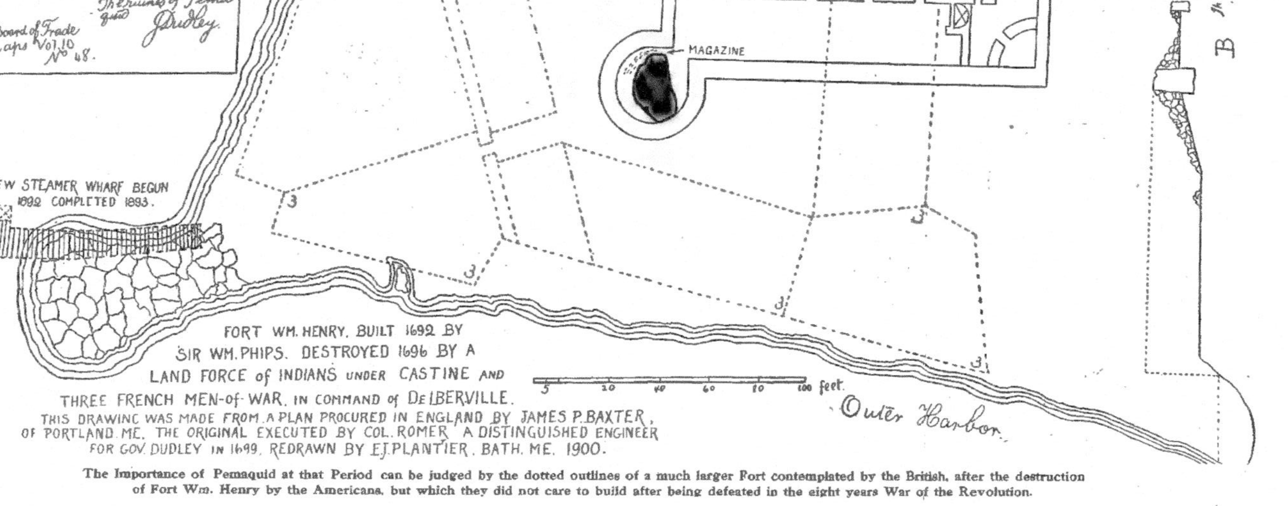

The Importance of Pemaquid at that Period can be judged by the dotted outlines of a much larger Fort contemplated by the British, after the destruction of Fort Wm. Henry by the Americans, but which they did not care to build after being defeated in the eight years War of the Revolution.

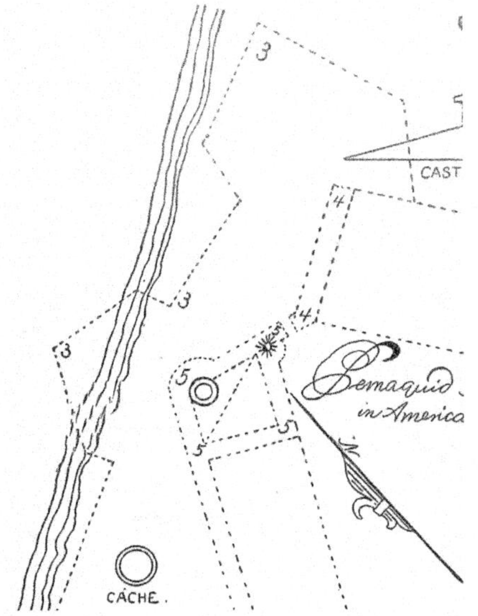
1 The Old Fort of Pemaquid.
2 The Barbican
3 The proposed new Fort
4 A Curtain or Espolement
to cover your
is proposed a Tower
staff a watch house Armory &
other conveniences. 1699
A The Fort as it was before the French
took and Demolished it
B The Profil as it now lyes in its Ruin
CAST
CACHE.
Pemaquid
in America

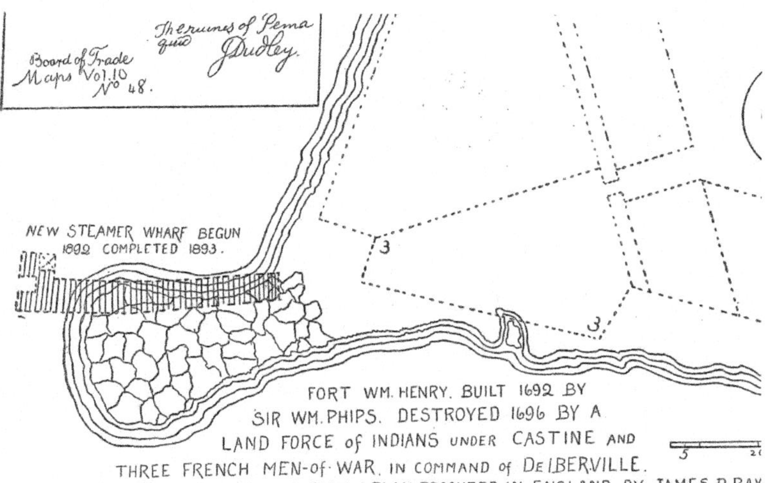

**The Importance of Pemaquid at that Period can be judged by the dotted outlin
of Fort Wm. Henry by the Americans, but which they did not care to bu**

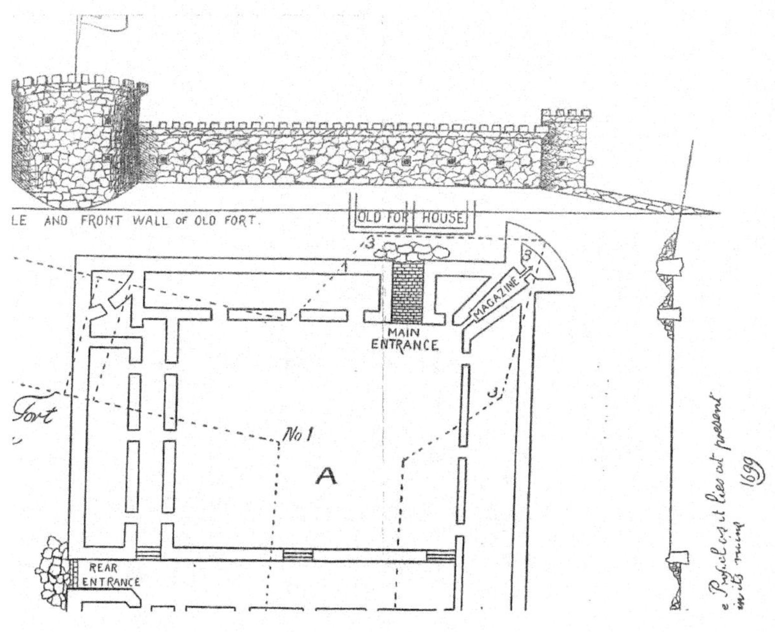

LE AND FRONT WALL OF OLD FORT.
OLD FORT HOUSE
MAGAZINE
MAIN ENTRANCE
REAR ENTRANCE
No 1
A
Fort

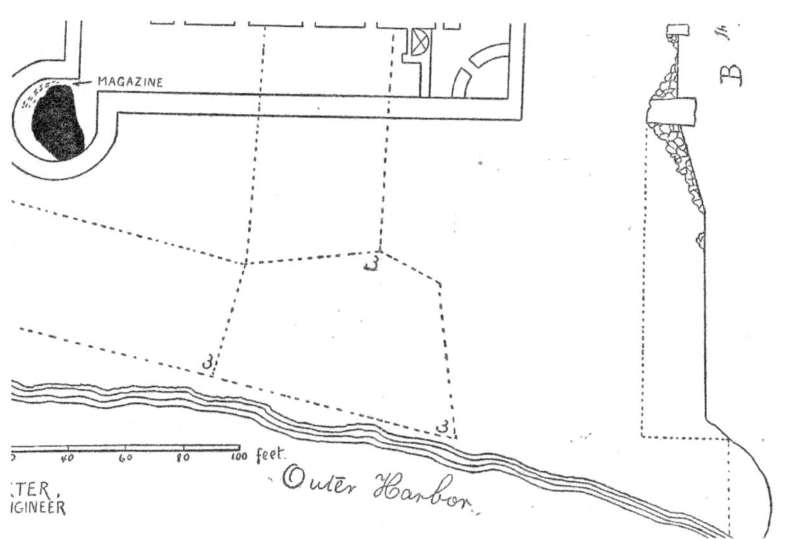

es of a much larger Fort contemplated by the British, after the destruction
ild after being defeated in the eight years War of the Revolution.

www.ingramcontent.com/pod-product-compliance
Lightning Source LLC
LaVergne TN
LVHW020539100826
845148LV00010B/1542
* 9 7 8 0 7 8 8 4 2 7 0 7 7 *